SCHOLASTIC GUIDES

Writing Winning Reports and Essays

Paul B. Janeczko

SCHOLASTIC
REFERENCE

For Terry and Cheryl Bowers,
who shared their home, their hearts. . .
and their big-screen TV with me.

Library of Congress Cataloging-in-Publication Data
Janeczko, Paul B.
Writing winning reports and essays/ Paul B. Janeczko.
p. cm. (Scholastic guides)
Summary: Provides strategies for writing successful research reports and essays,
including social studies reports, book reports, persuasive essays, personal essays,
and descriptive essays.
1. English language—Composition and exercises. 2. Essay—Authorship. 3. Report writing.
[1. English language—Composition and exercises. 2. Authorship. 3. Report writing.] I. Title.
II. Series
PE1408 .J425 2003
808'.042—dc21
2002030543

0-439-28717-0 (pob)
0-439-28718-9 (pb)
Book design by Kay Petronio
10 9 8 7 6 5 4 3 2 1   03 04 05 06 07
Printed in the U.S.A.   23
First printing, July 2003

Contents

4 | Contents

INTRODUCTION

I hope this guide helps you to be a better writer in school. I've tried to give attention to the types of writing that you may have to do for your classes. I start with a brief discussion of the writing process and the writer's notebook. You can't be a really good writer without paying attention to each stage of the writing process. The writer's notebook can turn out to be one of your best friends when it comes to writing, and I'll explain how it can help you.

Most of this guide is filled with practical advice and suggestions for improving your writing. Among other things, I explore how to get ideas for your reports and essays and how to organize your thoughts. I offer some suggestions for drafting and revising your reports and essays. I also give some tips on doing research and writing with style.

Like any guide, this one is designed to give you the confidence to succeed. It offers suggestions and advice that will help you write more organized and thoughtful reports and essays. It can also help you write with more flair. It's not meant to be a set of never-to-be-broken rules. This guide can help you in school when you need to write:

➡ a report for social studies or science class

➡ a report about a person or a place

➡ an essay that will persuade someone to your way of thinking about an issue

➡ a narrative about your life

➡ several types of book reports

Beyond what this guide can mean to your school writing, I hope it helps you be a better writer outside of class, because you're not going to be in school forever. If you learn to write clear and interesting prose, it can help you in your work, in your letters to family and friends, and in the personal writing that you do with no intention of ever showing it to another person. Sure, it's important to be a better writer for school. But it's far more important to write for *yourself*.

A FEW WORDS ABOUT
the Writing Process

Because I make a living writing and teaching writing to kids and adults, most people think that I was a good writer from a very early age. I wish these people could have seen when I was in elementary school and even in high school. When I was a kid, there were few things that I found as boring and as difficult as writing. The words *torture* and *agony* come to mind. I remember spending countless hours at our kitchen table or at my desk in school staring at the blank page, pencil clenched firmly in my fist, as if I could squeeze the words onto the page. Rather than winding up with some words on the page, I wound up with a cramp in my right hand.

Part of the problem was the way I was taught writing. I wasn't. I was taught grammar and spelling. But that's not writing. Oh, grammar and spelling are important to good writing, but long before you worry about those things you need to think about the words. I was given a topic — usually something boring, or at least something I didn't care about — told how long the paper needed to be and when it was due. The rest was up to me. I could feel the despair begin to build, and I'd not even begun to stare at the blank page. That would come later when I was seated at the table — the blue lines of the composition paper reminding me of the bars of a jail — wishing that a perfect theme would magically appear on the paper and I could escape outside to play.

My dread at having to write was matched by the sick feeling I got in my stomach when I remembered we were going to get our papers graded and returned to us. Mine were usually covered with red marks. Nothing helpful was marked on the paper. Just the things that I'd done wrong. Sometimes the paper didn't have any comments at all, except for the grade and a few words of advice, like "Try harder!" or "Watch your punctuation!" Not very helpful. I had no conferences about my papers, except with my buddies when we got together in the corner of the playground to complain. About the only rewriting I did was when my mother made me copy the paper over in neater penmanship.

One of the best things that has happened to young writers is that teachers have come to understand that writing is a process, and that the process is almost as important as the finished product. They've also come to understand that good writing takes time. Time to think and jot down notes. Time to doodle and draft, to confer, read aloud, and revise. Time to think, to revise more.

This process will not be the same for everyone. You may need more time to revise than your buddy, who has fewer things that need to be changed. But an important thing to always bear in mind is that if you do not go through the writing process, your writing will suffer. This is true if you are writing a report or an essay. It will not be as good as it can be. I don't know a single writer who writes anything great without rewriting. The old adage is true: Writing is rewriting.

For me, the most enjoyable part of writing, other than writing the draft, is the prewriting. I get out a yellow legal pad and one of my favorite pens, then start brainstorming. Brainstorming. I think that's the perfect word for this part of writing because it is when my brain is wild with ideas. Sometimes the ideas are loud like a thunderstorm. At other times they are much quieter, but persistent, like a spring snowfall. I just start writing them down. It doesn't matter if they are far-fetched. I make lists and draw diagrams. Maybe I'll draw a map. I may decide I need to interview someone. I may ask questions about different aspects of the topic. This might mean some research, something else I love about writing.

After the brainstorming comes writing the first draft. It took me a long time to realize that the first draft is . . . well, a first draft, which means that it won't be perfect. It may, in fact, be far from perfect. But that's to be expected. That's part of what the first draft is all about: giving yourself the chance to get your thoughts onto the page and not fretting if the writing isn't perfect. Your writing will get better as you revise and rewrite.

I'm a big fan of giving my writing a chance to sit alone out of sight for a while — a week or two, maybe longer — while I do other things. That gives me a chance to forget exactly what I've written. That way, when I come back to it, I can look at it with fresh eyes. You usually won't have as much time as I do to let your writing sit in a drawer. Nevertheless, by starting your writing assignment as soon as you can, you will have a bit of time to put it out of your mind before you begin to revise.

After you've had a chance to reread what you've written for the assignment, you'll probably see some parts that need improvement. Now is the time to make those changes, before you pass it on to a friend or writing partner for his comments. Once you've had time to discuss the paper, you must decide if you need to make more changes. Only after you have made the report as good as it can be are you ready to type the final copy and hand it to your teacher.

This writing process is essentially the same as the one that I go through when I write an article or a book. Sure, when I write a book, my process will be more intense and longer than yours. But the process is essentially the same, from the wild ride of brainstorming to the satisfaction of turning in a piece of writing that is as good as you can make it.

So, don't cheat yourself or your reader by handing in a report that you're not proud of. Take the time to let the writing process work for you. Be patient. Take the time to brainstorm, to write a draft, to revise. You may be surprised by what happens. You may not only write a wonderful report, but you'll have the satisfaction of seeing how good writing can be its own reward.

CHAPTER ONE

The Writer's Notebook

in 1969 as the brainchild
wanted to open a recordi
illage in upstate New Yo
Bob Dylan. The businessm
attract a lot of attention
ometown. Although they h
s to risk money on t
estors were interested
of this project that was
Music and Art Fe
Days of Peace a
accommodate
d the fair, t
e was move
nsidered whi
passing any "mu
lence" (American
peace singers like A
her acts were soon
rformers read like a
luding the Grateful
arwater Revival, and
o took pains to plan fo
ilities, and a medical st
t went into Woodstoc

In a letter to a friend, the great American poet Emily Dickinson said that the only commandment she faithfully kept was "Consider the lilies of the field." What she meant, of course, was that keeping her eyes open and observing the world around her were crucial to her writing. As you notice the details of your life, you may very likely come upon a topic that would make a fine report or essay. Noticing the colors of a sunset, for example, might lead to a topic for your science report. Noticing a pocketful of change might lead you to write a persuasive essay about the low wages of young workers. Your chances of writing an interesting report or essay are improved when you write about a topic that is important to you.

While observing life around you is necessary to good writing, you must do more than simply observe. You must record what you see and hear and feel and wonder. If you don't, you'll surely forget much of what you notice. I suspect that I'm a lot like you: I have many things on my mind. If I don't write them down, I forget. My writer's notebook helps me save my observations, but it also gives me the space to try out my feelings.

Every writer I know records his or her observations and reflections. Some scribble them down on scraps of paper or on the backs of old envelopes and grocery-store receipts. Others carry a small notebook. One poet I know — not to mention my own daughter — jots down his ideas on the palm of his hand! Another friend of mine carries a small voice recorder in her car so she can quickly save any thoughts without stopping the car to write them down. And even though these writers save their observations and notes as quickly as possible, nearly all of them have a larger writer's notebook that they add to on a regular basis. Some writers save their observations on a separate computer disk. This writer's notebook — whether it be paper or electronic — is a bank into which writers deposit their observations and feelings and questions, in order to draw on them later when they're ready to work on a piece of writing.

If you're truly interested in becoming a better writer, a first step that you could take would be to hustle down to the stationery store and buy a writer's notebook or set up a notebook file on your computer.

If you decide to use a paper notebook, what sort should you buy?

I'd suggest one with pages that are the size of the composition paper you use in school. If your pages are smaller than that, you might be reluctant to write down as much as you would like to. So, give yourself lots of space to fill with your words. I like to use a composition book with a stiff marbled cover. Other people prefer a spiral notebook. Still others have a three-ring binder. The writer's notebook is a tool that is supposed to help you and serve you. Choose a notebook that you are comfortable with— a notebook to which you look forward to returning regularly.

When should you make notes?

Before you forget the neat things. If you can, write as soon as you have something you want to save. That's not always practical, so that's why writers jot down ideas on their hands or on scraps of paper for safe-keeping until they can get to their notebooks or their computers. However, many writers, myself included, set aside some time every day to write in their notebooks. I like to write early in the morning when my house is quiet. Others like to write before they go to sleep. Do what works for you. You might want to set aside fifteen or twenty minutes every day to write in your notebook. That's one good habit to develop if you want to write better.

Don't expect to write something great every time you write in your notebook. Great writing comes with practice and revision. Just put your thoughts, feelings, and observations into words. Your notebook will become like a good friend who listens to you without interrupting or judging. Later, as you read through your notebook, don't be surprised if you find nuggets of writing that can become the heart of a longer piece of writing.

What should you write in your writer's notebook?

Simply put, write whatever strikes you. Anything you like. It's your book, so write in it things that you notice during the day or night. Things that are interesting, beautiful, exciting, disgusting. Things that make you laugh or cry. Snatches of overheard conversations. Your feelings about things and people and events. Write letters to friends, famous people, people you miss. Whatever you write need not "make sense" or be written in complete sentences. Lists, phrases, words are all fine things to add to your notebook. What do you notice through your senses? Details, like the hair that sticks out of your science teacher's nose, or the way your best friend's eyes crinkle when she smiles, or the sound of the floor creaking when your mother gets up early in the morning.

Of course, your writer's notebook is an ideal place for you to consider the "big questions" of life. Those questions that you ask yourself. Ones you might think about at night, trying to fall asleep. For instance: Why do good people have to suffer and die? What would make me happy? What kind of person would I like to be when I grow up? Why do things change? You don't even have to worry about writing an answer to these questions, because the important thing is thinking about them. But by considering these "big questions," you may very well come up with some ideas that you can write about in a more formal way.

I don't want to give the impression that your writer's notebook is just for writing. I know many writers, young and not so young, who include sketches, clippings, photographs, and other materials in their notebooks. I have no talent for drawing, but that doesn't stop me from making a sketch from time to time in my notebook. Maybe I'll draw a map of an area that I want to write a piece of fiction about or a picture of a shack that I stumbled across while I was walking through the woods. You might want to sketch a picture of a friend or your little sister, a sunset or an abandoned building, a swing set in a park or waves crashing on a beach. And don't forget that your sketches can be of imagined things and people, not just what you have actually seen.

In the pages of my notebook, I am more apt to tape newspaper and magazine clippings about topics that interest me, like baseball, art forgery, bird-watchers, and spies. Why these clippings? Because any one of them can help me when I am looking for a subject for a new nonfiction book. Or maybe a character in an article — like a gentlemanly bird-watcher — might be the basis for a fictional character.

A large part of one of my notebooks is a rogues' gallery, a collection of photographs and magazine pictures of people I know well or will never meet. Photos of my family and friends. News photos of the rich and famous. Faces from print ads. Regardless of who the person is, there is something about each face that fascinates me. Maybe a laugh line or a mustache or an eye patch. Maybe a sad look around the eyes. Sometimes I might write a few lines about a face, but more often than not I let each face tell its own story. And, of course, you can add pictures of nature scenes, city skylines, and animals. Whatever catches your eye.

How can a writer's notebook help you in school?

Your writer's notebook can be a valuable tool when it comes to selecting a topic for a report. I suggest you set aside a few pages for a topics menu, a place where you can jot down possible report topics, even the more far-fetched ones. If you hang on to your writer's notebook, with its notes and ideas, it can serve you as you move from grade to grade and need to write other reports.

Under your topic menu you can write down some questions that you wonder about. One of those questions might lead to a good paper. Here are some questions that interest me: Could the sinking of the *Titanic* have been avoided? Why is invisible ink invisible? How does a flower "work"? In other words, what process makes some flowers bloom, die off in the winter, then bloom again in warm weather? How much is a billion dollars? What could that amount of money buy?

If you keep your eyes open and let your imagination be free, you should have little trouble coming up with intriguing questions. Some will have clear answers, but others might have conflicting answers.

You can also write down things that would be fun to learn more about. For example:

➡ valuable baseball cards

➡ the life cycle of a sea turtle

➡ the disappearance of Amelia Earhart

➡ the Everglades

➡ automobiles of the future

Not every question or suggestion you write in your notebook will be a suitable report topic, but the point is to give yourself every chance to write about something that you're interested in. Then try to show your teacher that the topic you'd really like to write about would be a perfect topic for a report.

For example, if you are interested in the Everglades, you could easily write a science report on the ecosystem in the Everglades. Or you could write a report about the rare species of animals that live there. You could write a social studies report on efforts to save the Everglades from encroaching development. You could also write a social studies report about the Seminole Indians, who were the original inhabitants of the area.

If you're fascinated with Ben Franklin and his discovery of electricity, you might write a science report on that and some of his other inventions, like the lightning rod and the bifocal lens. You could also write a social studies report on Franklin the civil servant, the man who helped found a library, a fire company, a college, and a hospital. Or you could write a report on Franklin the politician and his work in England in the twenty years leading up to the American Revolution.

The point is that many topics can be looked at in different ways. So, if there is a topic that you'd really like to work with, look at it carefully to see if there is some aspect of it that you can research for a report for a particular school subject, like social studies or science.

If you think about it, your writer's notebook is like a treasure chest that is totally under your command. You put in it only that which strikes you. And you can look through this treasure chest whenever you want to. Like a true treasure chest, your writer's notebook will be filled with wonders and curiosities. As a writer, you can remove a few of the gems in your treasure chest and use them to help you write an essay or a report. If you work hard, your writing will shine as brightly as any of the treasures in your writer's notebook. But it will depend on how carefully you observe and how faithfully you record your questions and observations. There's no time to spare. Grab your notebook and a pencil, or set up a file on your computer, and start collecting your ideas and observations.

CHAPTER TWO

Writing a Report: A Basic Guide

in 1969 as the brainchild
vanted to open a recordi
illage in upstate New Yo
Bob Dylan. The businessm
attract a lot of attention
ometown. Although they h
s to risk money on t
estors were interested
of this project that was
Music and Art F
Days of Peace a
accommodate
d the fair, t
e was move
nsidered wh
passing any "mu
lence" (American
peace singers like A
her acts were soon
rformers read like a
cluding the Grateful D
arwater Revival, and J
o took pains to plan f
cilities, and a medical st
t went into Woodstoc

When you are writing a report for one of your classes, it will more than likely be based on research. In other words, it will require investigating your topic. Your research can be gathered from a number of sources:

Books, which include reference books, like encyclopedias and dictionaries, and circulating books from the library. You can even use your own books. If you have a strong interest in a subject, you may have a collection of books on that subject.

Periodicals, which include magazines, either popular titles like *Time* and *National Geographic*, or more specialized titles like publications of organizations and corporations.

The Web, which includes a staggering number of sources.

Interviews, which means that you gather information by asking questions of an expert on a subject.

Audiovisual sources, which include videos or recorded interviews with experts.

All the stages of a research report will require work. If you're impatient, you'll want to hurry through your research. Don't rush. Each step in the process of writing a report is important. When your teacher tells you that you need to research and write a report, it might seem like a lot of work. But if you break the process down into small steps, you will find that the job is easier. As you work on your report, remember one thing: The more effort you put into all the steps of the research process, the better your chances will be of writing a top-notch report.

Getting Ideas

In a perfect world, your teacher would allow you to choose your own topic for a report. Chances are, however, that there will be some restrictions. You might, for example, need to write about an American poet or about an issue related to cloning. Even though there may be such restrictions, let me offer two suggestions for selecting a topic for a report:

1. Choose a topic that interests you. I know that sounds pretty simple, but you'd be surprised how many students pick a topic because they think it is easy or because the topic is trendy. Often these students find themselves saddled with a topic that they find boring, and so it's sheer drudgery to research and write about.

2. Choose your topic as quickly as you can. Give it careful consideration, but choose quickly. If you don't, your choice may be limited because a classmate may have chosen the topic that you were interested in. Another reason to select your topic quickly is that the sooner you choose it, the sooner you can start working on it. Having more time to write the report means that you have a better chance of doing a good job on it.

Your topic can be something that you like, e.g., the origins of NASA or the life of a favorite writer or explorer. It can be about something that enrages you, like pollution or child abuse, yet compels you to find more information so you can be better informed. Or your topic can be something you're curious about, like Mount Rushmore. You might be interested in finding out how they decided which presidents to carve into the mountain. That might lead you to find out how they actually carved the monument.

What if your teacher assigns your report topic and gives you no say in the matter? I suggest that you take a little time to investigate the topic to see if you can find a way to modify it to make it more interesting for you. Your teacher may repay your efforts by allowing you to pursue the angle you have researched. However, if you are given a specific, narrow subject for your report with no chance to change it, there is, unfortunately, not much you can do about it except to make the best of it. Try to think of your report as a challenge to explore, to learn something new and fascinating, and to share your discoveries with others. Being angry at your teacher is only going to make the whole process that much more unpleasant for you. Trust me.

Once you have a topic, you need to make some decisions. Any "big" topic you can think about is too big for a short report like the one you will be asked to write. You need to find a way to narrow that subject. Otherwise, you will be writing vague general statements about your big topic. When you find the "small" topic, you will be able to find more interesting facts to include in your paper. But you must be careful not to get too small or you won't be able to find any facts about the topic! For example, if you want to write a report on Halley's comet, you may not be able to find a book on that subject. But if you look up "solar system" in the library catalog or in an encyclopedia, you will more than likely find some useful information. If you are going to write about the brain, you will want to consider books about human anatomy and the nervous system. Information about photosynthesis is found in books about cells and molecules. You would be smart to look in a book about birds for information about the osprey, but you might also look for information about birds of prey.

As you explore a subject, keep two things in mind:

1. You may need to narrow your subject. You couldn't, for example, write a good paper about animals or fish in general. You would need to narrow that to a particular kind of animal, like the bobcat, or a particular kind of fish, like the eel.

2. Even though you'll need a narrow subject to write a good report, you may need to expand your topic to find a wider category to which your specific topic belongs. For example, if you want to write about the hermit crab, be prepared to look for books and encyclopedia articles about crustaceans.

But, how do you get started if you have no idea what topic to write about? Or, what if your teacher gives you a general topic and expects you to find a narrow topic suitable for your report about that general topic? I will try to answer those questions in this section of the guide. I will take you through the entire research and writing process — from finding an idea to preparing your final copy — by showing how I researched and wrote "Why the United States Entered World War I," the writing model for a social studies report that appears at the end of this section. The subsequent sections of this guide will explore how to write other reports that you may be asked to write for one of your classes, from science reports to book reports. With a few slight variations, the process of writing other successful reports will be basically the same as the one I explain in this section.

Suppose your teacher announces that your report has to be about something in twentieth-century American history, but that it is up to you to find a suitably narrow topic. That means you need to choose some aspect of a subject that you can research sufficiently in a short period of time and write about thoughtfully in a few pages.

One way to discover a topic for your report is to browse the library shelves. For example, the social studies books are mostly in the 300s and the 900s (if your library uses the Dewey decimal system), so if you're writing a social studies report, start in one of those sections and look at the books that are on the shelves. For example, military-science books are numbered with 355. Criminology books are nearby in the 364 section. And if you look at books in the 385–388 section, you'll find books on all sorts of transportation. Books on ancient civilizations — the ones that existed in China, Egypt, and Greece — are in the 930–940 section. United States history books are in the 974–979 area. The more books you find on a certain topic, the better your chances of finding plenty of materials for your report.

Pull a couple of books from the shelves and thumb through them. You may find, for example, a photograph of the explosion of the Hindenburg in New Jersey in 1936 and decide to research the lighter-than-air aircraft. Or maybe you'll come across a chart showing the tallest structures in the ancient world and start thinking about how the pyramids were built. Chances are there is a topic just right for your report lurking in all those books in the library.

Another way to generate ideas is to create a writing "web," also called a "cluster." To begin your web, write the general topic in the center of the page. In this case, we write "20th-Century American History." Then let your mind go and see what ideas are related to that topic. You might want to look in your social studies book to get some ideas. A web might look like this:

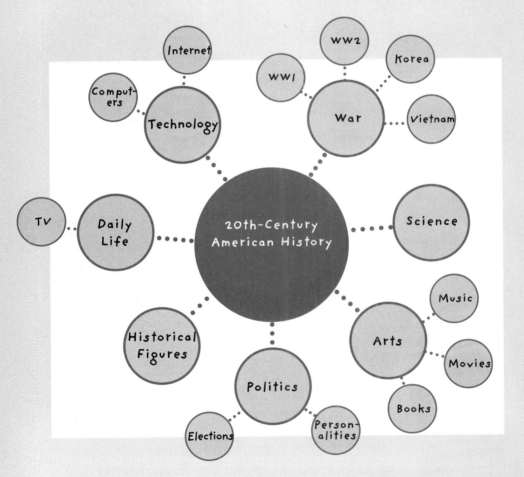

The next step is to look at those related topics and see if there is one that really gets your attention. Suppose you choose war. Write that topic at the center of a new web. Then repeat the process you just went through with the general topic. When you think of war, what elements come to mind? What questions do you have about war? Use those thoughts to create your new web, which might look like this:

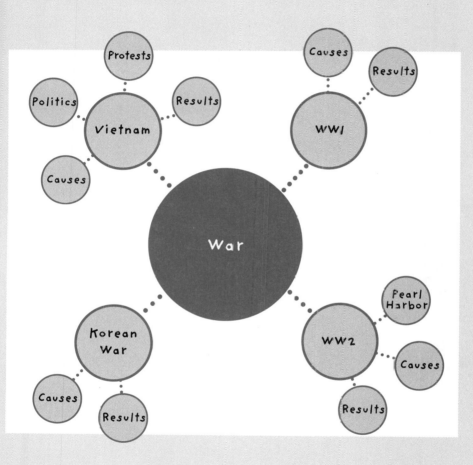

As you look at your new web, you might be most curious about World War I, since you watched a TV documentary that said many Americans were opposed to our country's involvement in a European war. And that might give you the angle for your report: Why did the United States enter World War I? Once you have your teacher's approval of the topic, you are ready to begin your investigation.

How to Take Notes

The notes you take for your report will go a long way toward determining whether you write an outstanding report or one that is merely okay. The better your notes, the better your chances of writing an outstanding report. At this point, you might have this question about taking notes: Where's the best place to write your notes?

Some people write their notes in a spiral notebook. They feel that this makes it less likely that they will lose them. There's some merit to that belief. However, I believe that it is better to take notes on 3"x 5" index cards. I say this because they give you something that notes in a notebook cannot give you: flexibility. You can easily shuffle and rearrange your cards in a way that reflects the way you are going to organize your paper. In fact, once you have organized your note cards, you can use that arrangement to write your outline.

The first thing you should do when you start taking notes is to write a source card for the first source you are taking notes from. For example, if your first source is a book, you need to write the name of the book and its author on your source card. You also need to record the name of the publisher, the city where the publisher is located, and the copyright year. All of this information is found on the first couple of pages of the book. If your source is a magazine article, you'll need to include the page numbers that the article appeared on, as well as the title of the article and the name and issue of the magazine. (Later, I will show you how to site other sources.)

Once you have written down all the relevant information about a source, write "#1" on your first source card in the upper right corner of the card. Your next source card will be #2, and so on. This number is important because it's a code number that you'll write on every note card with information from that same source. By putting the source-book number on your note cards, you will avoid having to write the title or the author of the book on every card. This is important. Don't forget to write your source number on each note card. There are few things more annoying than finding a note card and having no idea where those notes came from.

Why do you need this source information? You'll need it when you write the bibliography for your report, which is a list of the materials you used to find information. Such a list will allow your teacher to check your sources. But the bibliography also gives other readers of your report a starting point if they're interested in the same topic and want to explore it further.

Where should you look for information for your report? Begin your investigation by looking in an encyclopedia because encyclopedias are a good source of general information. After you've found some general information about your topic, you can go to books and magazines that will give you more specific information.

What do you write down for notes? You're looking for information that will help you answer the guiding question of your report: Why did the United States enter World War I? As you take notes, you'll be looking only for information that may help you answer that question. If you're not sure if a certain tidbit of information will help you, write it down. Even if you wind up not using it in your report, you're better off having too much information than too little. Since you're not sure exactly what you'll need, you'll more than likely wind up with more notes than you'll ever use. That's okay. If you don't take enough notes, you'll need to go back and do more research later, when you don't have as much time and should be moving on to the next step.

Your note-taking should be selective and economical. In other words, you'll write down as much information as you think might be helpful, but do it in as few words as possible rather than copying whole pages of notes. This will give you just the bare facts and allow you to put those facts in your own words in your report.

Many students think that the way to write a good report is to copy long passages from an encyclopedia and claim it as their own work. That's not writing a report. In fact, it's called plagiarism when you copy someone else's work and say that it's your own. It's cheating. It's against the law. Since you're writing about a subject that you more than likely know very little about, of course you will need to get information from other sources. Your teacher understands that. But there is a way to be careful about what you copy, and there is a way to give credit to the person who wrote the book or article from which you got your information. I will say more about that later.

Making a Schedule

One of the most important things you can do to help yourself write a good report is to make sure you plan your time carefully. This means that you should give yourself enough time to get an idea, research the idea, write the draft, and write the final report. If you don't, you will wind up being rushed and your report will suffer.

Pay careful attention to any schedule your teacher gives you, either on an assignment sheet or written on the board. Pay particular attention to all the deadlines that might be part of the report process. For example, you might have a "due date" for selecting your topic, handing in your outline, turning in your note cards, handing in the rough draft, and handing in the final copy of your report. Mark all those days down on a calendar. Don't just glance at the dates and say to yourself, "Oh, I'll remember them." You won't. Trust me. Write them down on a calendar so you can easily see the days you have between each due date.

Once you've written your dates on the calendar, notice what's due when and how much time you'll have for each part of your report. Then comes the important part: Start working right away. Don't put it off. Start finding a topic. Stick to your schedule, which means that you must spend some time each week working on your report and following your schedule.

A Few Words About Encyclopedias

Research Tip

Although the encyclopedia sets are found in the same section of the library and they look alike — all those fat, uniform volumes — they are not alike. The same is true for online and CD-ROM encyclopedias. For instance, if you look up "World War I" in *The World Book* and *Encyclopedia Americana*, you'll find some interesting differences.

The World Book article is fourteen pages long and ends with the kind of valuable material that might save me some time and work as I investigate my topic. This material includes the following:

→ A list of related articles found in the encyclopedia. The list is divided into significant topics, such as "Battle Areas," "Allied Military Biographies," and "Treaties."

→ An outline of the entire World War I article, which gives me the chance to see the whole article at a glance and helps me see where the information I need might be in the article.

→ About a dozen questions about World War I that can help me get the most out of the article but also may give me a good idea for a topic for a report. Here are a few of those questions in my own words: "What were the four chief causes of World War I? Which World War I heads of government made up the Big Four? Which countries formed the Triple Entente? The Triple Alliance? How did the two alliances differ?"

→ Additional resources, which is a list of books about "the war to end all wars."

The article in *Encyclopedia Americana* is about ten times longer than the article in *The World Book*. Although the information in both articles is arranged in chronological order, this one includes an outline at the beginning (perhaps a more helpful location), giving an overview of the article. The only material at the end of the articles is a list of books about World War I.

Your first instinct in researching a subject in an encyclopedia might be to grab the volume that contains your subject. In the case of my example, grabbing the encyclopedia volume with "World War I" might be the way to start doing research. However, looking in the index volume of the encyclopedia can save time and work. Each set of encyclopedias has one volume — the last — that is an index of all the books in the set. And just as the articles in these encyclopedias are different, the same is true for the index in the last volume of each set.

As you might expect, because the article in *Encyclopedia Americana* is so much longer than the one in *The World Book*, its index entry for World War I is more detailed. Not only is it longer, but its headings are more helpful for a researcher looking for information on a particular aspect of a large subject like World War I. For example, there are headings like "Armaments," "Historical Background," and "Naval Operations." And, to help with my question — "Why did the United States enter the war?" — there is the heading "Neutrality and Neutral Nations," with listings for "*Lusitania*" and "United States." A quick look through the list of topics shows that there is a reference to the "Zimmermann note." Although I didn't know what the Zimmermann note is, I know it is related to World War I, so I need to investigate it. The index notations in *The World Book* are in alphabetical order and include "Neutrality" but no listing for *Lusitania* or the Zimmermann note.

Before you plunge into a search of a general encyclopedia, it is important to take a few minutes to see how the articles are set up in the book. There might very well be subheadings, an outline, or a list of questions that would let you narrow your search, which will save you time.

General encyclopedias include:

Academic American Encyclopedia

Collier's Encyclopedia

Compton's Encyclopedia
Encyclopedia Americana
Encyclopedia Britannica
The World Book Encyclopedia

In addition to these general encyclopedias, there are also a number of specialized encyclopedias that might help you with other research. These titles will give you an idea of the topics that are covered in each:

The Cutting Edge: An Encyclopedia of Advanced Technologies
Disney A to Z: The Official Encyclopedia
Encyclopedia of Computer Science
Encyclopedia of Native American Tribes
Encyclopedia of North American Trees
The Encyclopedia of Phobias, Fears, and Anxieties
Encyclopedia of Television
The New Encyclopedia of the Cat
Oh Yuck! The Encyclopedia of Everything Nasty
The Oxford Encyclopedia of the Modern Islamic World
Scholastic Encyclopedia of the Presidents
Scholastic Encyclopedia of Women in the United States

Taking Notes

Let us say that you've already looked at the articles in *The World Book Encyclopedia* and *Encyclopedia Americana*. You own the *Grolier Multimedia Encyclopedia* on a CD-ROM, and that's where you decide to start your formal research and look up "World War I." You'll also consult other encyclopedias if you find it necessary, but for starters you think that the CD-ROM would be a reliable source for general information about World War I.

As you expect, there is a long article about the subject. However, because you're only interested in how the United States got involved in the war, you don't need to read the whole article, especially since it is nicely divided into small sections with helpful headings. Although you're specifically interested in how the United States entered World War I, you want to have some basic background about how the war got started and which countries were fighting each other. Before you take any actual notes, write out a source card:

Grolier Multimedia Encyclopedia   [#1]
CD-ROM edition, 1998

Notice the #1 in the right hand corner of the card. That is the code number you'll write on every card on which you take notes from this source. As I explained earlier, this saves you the trouble of having to write out the name of the book every time you fill out a new note card.

As you read the beginning of the article, you find the information that you are looking for and write it in your own words on a card. After you write your notes, try to summarize them in a few words on the top line of the note card. It is very important to write on the top of each card a brief summary of the material that is on that card. This heading will help you organize your note cards and write an outline for your report. It will save you time and help you write a more detailed outline.

Here are some sample note cards:

The start of the war   [#1]

-Assassination of Austrian archduke Franz Ferdinand in
    Sarajevo in 1914 starts the war in Europe

> Taking sides [#1]
>
> -Triple Entente: Great Britain, France, and Russia vs.
>   Triple Alliance: Germany, Austria-Hungary, and Italy
>
> -U.S. interests lie with Entente

These two note cards seem to give you the basic information that you were looking for. But to find out about the role of the United States in the war, you need to look further. You carefully scroll through Part 1 of the article, looking for subheadings that might mention the United States. You find nothing that looks helpful. However, when you scan Part 2 of the article, you find a section marked "United States Entry." As you read the opening paragraph, you find information that you think will find a place in your report, and you write down some notes:

> U.S. neutral [#1]
>
> -President Wilson declares that the U.S. would be neutral
>   in the war, even though his advisers and many citizens
>   want the U.S. to help its allies

From the next paragraph, you take these notes:

> Eng. and Ger. battle for Atlantic [#1]
>
> -England blockades Germany
>
> -Germany establishes a "war zone" around Eng.; says it
>   will sink all ships in the area
>
> -By mid-1915, few ships sink; few American lives lost

Notice that you put quotations marks around "war zone" to show that they were taken directly from the text. Notice, too, that you used a sort of shorthand — "Eng." for "England" and "By mid-1915" instead of "By the middle of 1915" — to cut down on the writing. Such shortcuts are helpful in your notes, as long as you understand your own abbreviations.

In the third paragraph of the article, you find the first reason why the U.S. finally entered the war:

> Ger. sinks ships; lives lost   [#1]
>
> - Ger. subs sink *Lusitania*; many lives lost
>
> -Wilson protests to Ger.
>
> -Arabic sinks
>
> -Ger. agrees to stop sinking passenger ships
>
> -Ger. sinks *Sussex*
>
> -Ger. agrees again to stop sinking ships

The next paragraph is about President Wilson's popularity, but mentions nothing about the war. The following paragraph, however, is filled with important information, so you start writing notes:

> Ger. subs   [#1]
>
> -Ger. announces it will resume "unrestricted submarine warfare"
>
> -Wilson breaks off diplomatic relations with Ger.

Zimmermann telegram   [#1]

-Arthur Zimmermann, Ger. foreign minister, sends secret
  note to Mexico govt.

-Zimm. asks that Mexico attack Texas, New Mexico &
  Arizona if U.S. enters the war against Ger.

-This will keep U.S. occupied and not able to send troops
  to Europe

-Note angers Wilson and citizens

More sinkings   [#1]

-Ger. sinks more U.S. ships

-U.S. in war   [#1]

-Congress declares war on Ger., 4/6/17; on Austria-
  Hungary, 12/7/17

By the time you've gone through the article on your CD-ROM encyclopedia, you have a basic understanding of why the United States
entered the war. And you can see from your notes that your report will
probably be written in chronological order. In other words, how the
events happened. However, as you look at your notes, you realize that
you don't have any notes on what led up to the start of the war other than
the assassination of Archduke Ferdinand. You turn to *The World Book
Encyclopedia* for help and find it near the beginning of the article. You
write out a source card:

World War I   [#2]

The World Book Encyclopedia

Vol. 21, pp. 452–467

Then you write out your note card:

Main reasons for war   [#2, p. 452]

-The main reasons for the war were

(1) a rise of nationalism, (2) buildup of military might,
(3) competition for colonies, (4) a system of military
alliances

But you can tell you need more information because you still have some questions that you need to answer. As you think of these questions, you write them down in your notebook:

NEED TO FIND OUT

When did the *Lusitania* sink?

How many Americans died in the sinking?

When did Wilson end relations with Germany?

What did Mexico expect to get out of going to war
   against the U.S.?

How did President Wilson and the American people find
   out about the Zimmermann telegram?

How did Wilson and the American people feel about going
   to war with Germany?

Writing down questions that still need to be answered after your initial research is an important part of writing a report. For one thing, it is a way to think through the topic. Writing a report is something like putting together a jigsaw puzzle. You need to have all the pieces in place to give you and your reader the complete picture. Writing down unanswered questions will help you focus your research and find the final pieces of your report.

To find the answers to these questions, you need to investigate other resources. It's always a good idea to have a number of sources for a report. Teachers generally won't accept reports in which the information came from a single source, like an encyclopedia.

Since you are looking for information about why the U.S. entered World War I and not merely general information about the war, you need to look for a book about American history. A quick check of the catalog at the library offered many possibilities. You selected *A History of the American People,* by Samuel Eliot Morison.

You first consult the index, looking for a reference to the *Lusitania*. Surprisingly, there were none. You can't stop there. You need to investigate further, so you check the table of contents to see if you can find the spot where the author talks about World War I. Sure enough, there are three sections that look like they might be helpful. But you notice that one chapter has a section called "Neutrality Problems." You turn to it and quickly skim the pages looking for reference to the *Lusitania*. There are only a few lines about the ship, but they contain information that you are looking for.

Once you know you are going to use this book, write out a source card:

A History of the American People	[#3]
Samuel Eliot Morison	
New York: Oxford Univ. Press, 1965	
call # 973 M68h	

Since this is a library book, you include its call number, just in case you need to double-check some information.

With your source card written and numbered, you then write the important information on one note card:

> *Lusitania* [#3, p. 852]
>
> -Sinks off coast of Ireland
>
> -May 7, 1916
>
> -1,100 dead; 128 Americans, including women

As long as you have this history book, you check the index to see if there is any information on the Zimmermann telegram. There is, so you quickly flip to page 858 to see if there is anything you can use. You find nothing helpful in the paragraph on the infamous telegram.

Since you still have a few unanswered questions, you look for another American history book. You locate one, check the index, and see a reference to the Zimmermann note. You find the page and quickly read the paragraph about the Zimmermann telegram. Much to your delight, you find some of the exact words that were in the original intercepted message. You write out a source card:

> *The American Nation* [#4]
>
> John D. Hicks, George E. Mowry, Robert E. Burke
>
> Boston: Houghton Mifflin Co., 1963
>
> call # 973 H631f

Then you copy down the words from the telegram:

> Zimmermann telegram [#4, pp. 4C4–5]
>
> - Words of Z. to president of Mexico: "That we shall make war together and together make peace. We shall give generous financial support and it is understood that Mexico is to re-conquer the lost territory in New Mexico, Texas, and Arizona."

At this point, you feel pretty good about your research. You have consulted a CD-ROM encyclopedia and two history books to find some important information that you hope to include in your report. But before you can think about starting to organize your notes, you need to make sure you've covered all the bases. You look back in your notebook to the few questions you wrote down after you'd done your initial research in the encyclopedia. You've answered all but two of your questions: "How did Wilson and the American people feel about going to war with Germany?" and "How did President Wilson and the American people find out about the Zimmermann telegram?"

To answer your remaining questions, you decide to look for books about World War I. The card catalog lists a couple that seem promising: *The American Heritage History of World War I* and *A Short History of World War I*. With note cards at the ready, you take a closer look at these books and find some information that needs to be noted. You write out source cards and take some notes:

> *The American Heritage Book of World War I* [#5]
>
> Editors of American Heritage magazine
>
> New York: Simon & Schuster, 1964
>
> call # 940.3 M369

Zimmermann telegram   [#5, p. 204]

-Admiral Sir William R. Hall, head of British code
   breakers, decides to hold off notifying Wilson about Z.
   note

-After Wilson cuts diplomatic ties with Ger., Hall sends
   decoded message to President

-Wilson outraged by Ger. plan

-March 1, Z. telegram "made headlines all over the United
   States"

A Short History of World War I   [#6]

James L. Stokesbury

New York: William Morrow & Co., 1981

call # 940.3 S874s

Zimmermann telegram   [#6, p. 221]

-Hall decides to "sit on this juicy bit of stupidity until
   the time was ripe."

-Releases it on Feb. 25

Wilson and war   [#6, p. 22]

-Wilson is elected by a "fairly narrow margin" of 6 million
  votes out of a total of 17 million

-Campaign slogan: "He kept us out of war."

To find more information about the Zimmermann telegram you decide that you need to do some online searching. You fire up your browser, find the site for *Encyclopedia Britannica* (www.britannica.com), and search for "Zimmermann telegram." Within seconds, on the screen in front of you, you see that one of your choices is "Zimmermann, Arthur." Knowing that this was the name of the German minister, you click on that link. Before you can say "Zimmermann telegram," the screen shows an encyclopedia entry for Arthur Zimmermann. You read the entry and find what you are looking for. You write out a source card

britannica.com   [#7]

"Zimmermann, Arthur"

Then you jot down your notes:

Zimmermann telegram   [#7]

-Intercepted and decoded by British Admiralty
  intelligence

-Given to Wilson

-Publishes it on March 1, 1917

You still have one unanswered question: "When did Wilson end relations with Germany?" After a quick scan of the article in *Encyclopedia Americana*, you find the section that you think will give you the answer. You read carefully and find your answer. So, you write out a source card and a note card:

"World War I"   [#8]

Encyclopedia Americana

Vol. 29, pp. 216–363

Relations with Germany   [#8, p. 335]

-"Wilson, in view of his earlier pronouncements, had no
    choice except to sever diplomatic relations, and he did
    so on February 3, 1917."

With this note card, you figure that you have all the information you need to write a good social studies report. But before you go on to the second part of the process, you read over your notes to see if there is any other information that you need to find. Of course, there's always the possibility that when you start writing your report, you will find a gap in your research that may need to be filled. But, when you read over your notes, you are satisfied that you are ready to begin organizing your notes into an outline.

Getting Organized

Your teacher may ask you to write and submit an outline for your report. A lot of students think that it's not necessary to write an outline before they write their reports. In a way, they're right. Plenty of students have written reports without writing outlines. But, while it might not be necessary to write an outline before you write your report, it could help you write a better report than you could write without one. So, even if your teacher does not require you to hand in an outline, it's a good idea to write one anyway. Knowing how to organize a body of information in an outline is a skill that can help you in high school on the SATs and the achievement tests, when you have to write an essay from a given body of facts.

How can writing an outline help you write a better report? By giving you the chance to organize your thoughts and facts before you start writing the report itself. Also, it will show you if you need to do more research to fill in any gaps in the report. The more thought and work you put into your outline, the easier it will be to write your report. Consider the time spent planning and writing an outline to be time well spent.

Many students who complain about writing an outline for a report probably haven't taken very good notes, because the more complete your notes are, the easier it is to write a good outline. If you have followed my suggestions about taking notes, especially the one about writing the topic in a few words on the top of a note card, writing an outline shouldn't be very difficult.

First of all, read over all your notes. If there are parts that are unclear to you, correct them, even if it means going back to the source of those notes. Next, look over the topics you've written at the top of each card and make a separate pile for all note cards that have similar or related topics written at the top. Each pile could wind up being a separate part of your report.

As you look back over the notes that you took for your report, you see that there are three main categories of notes: the war in Europe, German submarine warfare, and the Zimmermann telegram. However, when you looked more carefully at your notes, you see that two of those categories — German submarine warfare and the Zimmermann telegram — can be divided into two parts. You can also see that there was a chronological progression of events. In other words, there were things that happened in a sequential order that led the United States into the war. So, as you suspected from the beginning, organizing your paper in chronological order makes sense.

The first draft of your outline look like this:

I.   Introduction.

II. Europe at war.

III. Early German submarine warfare.

IV. Later German submarine warfare.

V.   Zimmermann telegram intercepted.

VI. Zimmermann telegram revealed to U.S. and world.

VII. Conclusion.

Because each section of an outline represents one paragraph, it looks like the report will be six paragraphs long.

As you work on your outline, it's important to remember that not every topic that you wrote on the top of your note cards will necessarily become a part of the outline. For example, notes on the *Lusitania* were included in the section on early German submarine warfare. And some of your note cards just might not fit, after all, into the topic you chose. And you don't want to include information in your report that doesn't connect to your topic.

To take this rough draft of the outline to the next stage, you need to write each main point as a complete sentence. Then, under each main point you add your support for that point. When you add the supporting details, your outline looks like this:

I. Introduction.

II. World War I spreads quickly across Europe.

    A. Causes of the war in Europe.

    B. The assassination of Archduke Franz Ferdinand.

    C. Battle lines quickly drawn.

    D. Wilson keeps the U.S. out of the war.

    E. Events change that.

III. Early German warfare angers many in the U.S

    A. England blockades Germany.

    B. Germany creates war zone for subs.

    C. Germany sinks several ships; some U.S. deaths.

    D. *Lusitania* sinks, killing 128 Americans.

    E. Germany pays damages for losses.

    F. Germany stops sinking unarmed ships.

IV. Germany changes its submarine policies.

    A. Germany resumes "unrestricted submarine warfare."

    B. Wilson breaks diplomatic ties with Germany.

    C. Many Americans want war.

    D. Wilson resists.

V. Zimmermann telegram involves Mexico.

    A. Telegram intercepted and deciphered by British.

    B. Germany plans to ask Mexico to fight U.S.

> C. Germany returns New Mexico, Arizona, Texas to Mexico.
> VI. Zimmermann telegram is made public.
> A. At first British hold on to telegram.
> B. Wilson breaks ties with Germany.
> C. British send telegram to Wilson.
> D. Wilson is outraged.
> E. Wilson makes telegram public.
> F. Congress declares war on Germany on April 6, 1917.
> G. Congress declares war on Austria-Hungary eight months later.
> VII. Conclusion.

As you look at this outline, notice two things:

1. The main points — those with the Roman numerals — are the categories into which you divided your note cards (based on the topics that you'd written at the top of each note card).

2. The paper follows a chronological order, from the assassination of the archduke in 1914 to the U.S. Congress declaring war three years later.

There are other ways to organize your research. For example, you could write it as a persuasive essay (see page 171). You could also write it as a problem-solution report (see page 183). For this report on World War I, writing in chronological order is the way to go because it gives you an easy path to follow as you write the report, and when you do a good job of it, the reader will also be able to easily follow that same path.

You'll notice that the outline begins with a section called "Introduction" and ends with a section called "Conclusion." Whatever comes in between these opening and closing parts is called the "body" of your report. Do you need an introduction and conclusion in your report? Absolutely. What should you write in your introduction and conclusion? Although it might seem obvious from the names of these parts of your report, the introduction introduces the topic of your report to your reader, and the conclusion smoothly concludes your report. Let me explain what that means.

The introduction to your report should get the reader's attention so that she wants to continue reading it. You might do as I did in my sample report (page 48) and ask a question as part of your introduction. The question I asked is, Why would our country enter a war that was being fought on the other side of the Atlantic? The body of my sample report answers that question. You might also tell some sort of anecdote that is related to your topic and use that story as a way of getting into the body of your report. For example, if you were writing about Beethoven, you might tell the story of how difficult it was for you at times when you were taking piano lessons, but then you got to thinking about how incredible it was for Beethoven, who was deaf, to compose so much wonderful music. From there you could move into your report about the life of this German composer.

Your conclusion should relate to your introduction in some way. In my sample report, for example, I conclude by saying that because of several events and actions that I explained in my report, President Wilson could not keep our country out of war, even though that war took place far from American soil. Getting back to my example in the previous paragraph about a report of Beethoven, you could conclude by writing something about how you came to respect and admire the music of Beethoven as you learned more about him.

The body of your paper will be, by far, the largest part of your report. It will be four or five paragraphs, maybe longer. The introduction and the conclusion will be much shorter, but you should pay close attention to them nonetheless because they will make your report appear complete.

Writing the Draft

When I write an article or a report, it helps to visualize the project as a funnel. The wide part of the funnel is the beginning of the process, where I have all these ideas floating around in my head and a stack of books and other material from which I hope to find the information that will make for a good report. The funnel gets narrower as I do my research and select the right information for the report. As I write the draft, the funnel gets narrower still because I refine my notes into a form that my audience will be able to follow and understand. The final draft of my report is the narrowest part of the funnel because that is when I am left with only the most important information written in the clearest, sharpest way I can.

When you get to this part of the writing process, you'll probably notice that you have already spent a lot of time on the report but haven't even written a single word of the first draft! You should pat yourself on the back for not having taken the easy way out. Remember the good news: All this early work should make it easier for you to write a good report. Honest. With your notes and outline in hand, you are ready to write your draft.

As you face that task, keep one thing in mind: You're writing a draft and shouldn't expect it to be perfect. If you are careful, your draft may turn out to be pretty good. But it will still need some tinkering and revising, so don't try to get it perfect. That just puts too much pressure on you. Just write as well as you can. Thoughtful revision will make the report better.

But as you write your first draft, this is a good time to remind yourself that you need to give credit in your paper to all the information that you have found in other sources, like encyclopedias, books, and magazines. This means information that you quote directly from a source in your report, but it also means information from other sources that you put into your own words. Material you quote word for word, whether it be a few words or a few sentences, will, of course, be included in quotation marks.

Chances are that your teacher will ask you to give source credits within the body of the work. This means that you will include the author's last name and the page number on which you found the information. This notation will be written in parentheses and placed at the end of the information you obtained from that source, whether it be a direct quotation or a summary of information. If you read the first paragraph of my report draft that follows, you will notice my references to where I found information: *Grolier*, a CD-ROM encyclopedia with no page numbers and no specific author (because there are none in this CD encyclopedia) and Stokesbury, 221. To find out which book by Stokesbury I used, readers will turn to the very last page of the report, where they'll find the bibliography, a list of all my sources.

I'll have more to say about the bibliography later (see page 55), but here are the basics of how to include source information in your text: If your information comes from a book with a single author, you refer to it in your report by author and page number, e.g., Stokesbury, 221; if the book or magazine article has no author, you can refer to the title of the book or magazine, e.g., *The New York Times*. You need not include page numbers for CD-ROM sources, e.g., *Grolier Multimedia Encyclopedia*. As you read through the first draft of my report, note how I give credit to the books and the CD-ROM in which I found my information.

One final word about giving credit to your sources. You do not need to give a reference for information that is considered common knowledge, even though you may have read that information in a book. For example, if you are doing a report on George Washington and you read in an encyclopedia that he was our first president and has become known as the "Father of Our Country," you would not need to give credit to the encyclopedia for those two tidbits of information because they are considered common knowledge, something that is generally known.

WHY THE UNITED STATES ENTERED WORLD WAR I
by Paul B. Janeczko

Everybody knows that World War I was the first war of the twentieth century. It involved many European nations, as well as Russia. The United States did not enter the war until it had been raging for a few years. Why would our country enter a war that was being fought on the other side of the Atlantic? As you might imagine, the answer to that question is not a simple one.

World War I started in 1914, following the assassination of Archduke Franz Ferdinand of Austria. Before very long, all of Europe was fighting. Germany, Austria-Hungary, and Italy were on one side; Great Britain, France, and Russia, on the other. As the war continued, President Woodrow Wilson managed to keep the United States out of it (*Grolier*). In fact, when Wilson was elected for a second term in 1916, his campaign slogan boasted, "He kept us out of war" (Stokesbury, 221). However, several things that happened during the war left Wilson with no choice but to commit the United States to what became known as the Great War.

One of the reasons the United States entered the war was German submarine warfare. When England blockaded German ports, Germany declared a "war zone" around England and warned everybody to stay out of this area (*Grolier*). A few ships were sunk, and a

← **When?**

← **Who?**

few American lives were lost. But Americans were surprised when the British ship *Lusitania* was torpedoed ← Better word?
and sunk off the coast of Ireland. Nearly 1,100 people ← When?
were killed, including 128 Americans (Morison, 852).
President Wilson protested to Germany against this act, ← When?
and Germany agreed to pay some of the monetary
damages for the loss of ships and lives. It also agreed to
stop sinking unarmed ships (*Grolier*).

    Things changed when Germany announced it would ← When?
resume "unrestricted submarine warfare." Wilson
responded by breaking off diplomatic relations with
Germany in February (*Grolier*). More and more
Americans were calling for Wilson to declare war. He
resisted. But not for long.

    The British intercepted and deciphered a telegram ← When?
from Arthur Zimmermann, the German foreign
minister, to the German minister in Mexico. The
telegram wanted the Mexicans to enter the war on
Germany's side. If it did, the United States would be so
involved with fighting on its southern border that it
would not be able to enter the war on the side of the
British (*American Heritage*, 203). The so-called
Zimmermann telegram offered Mexico money and land ← Be specific.
if it declared war against the United States (Hicks, 404).
    Admiral Sir William R. Hall, the head of British
code-breakers, decided to hang on to this "juicy bit of
stupidity until the time was right" (Stokesbury, 221). He
didn't have to wait long. When Wilson got mad at

Germany, Hall sent the Zimmermann telegram to the president. Needless to say, Wilson was shocked by Germany's plan. On March 1, the Zimmermann telegram "made headlines all over the U.S." (Stokesbury, 221). A month later, on April 6, 1917, Congress declared war on Germany. By the end of the year, it declared war on Austria-Hungary.

Although President Wilson was able to keep the United States out of the Great War for several years, the actions of Germany made it impossible for the United States to remain neutral. Germany's unrestricted submarine warfare and its plan to involve Mexico in the war proved more than the president and Congress could stand. The United States went to war in Europe.

When I reread my draft, I thought the writing was pretty good. What I liked most about it was that I kept things in the proper chronological order, something that is very important to this report. However, as I read over the draft, I noticed that I was a little short on dates. In other words, although the events were in their proper places, I needed to be more specific about when they took place. I have marked those spots with a boldface "**When?**" in the margin: When did England blockade German ports? When did the *Lusitania* sink? When did Germany resume "unrestricted submarine warfare"? Can I be more specific about when the British intercepted the Zimmermann telegram? At this point, I looked back through my notes and found more specific dates for all three events.

One of the ways to make your report come alive is to include interesting quotations from experts. In my draft, I liked the way I included Hall's quote that the intercepted telegram was a "juicy bit of stupidity."

On the other hand, I felt that saying that Germany offered Mexico "money and land" was a bit flat. Turning to my notes again, I found the exact words in the Zimmermann telegram and saw exactly what Germany did offer Mexico: "generous financial support and it is understood that Mexico is to re-conquer the lost territory in New Mexico, Texas, and Arizona." Another good quote to include in my report.

While having the correct dates and including some critical quotations are very important in a report, so is the writing. I needed to read through my draft again, looking closely at the writing. As you can see, I have marked a number of places where I think the writing is flat or sloppy, places where strong verbs or more precise adjectives can breathe more life into the report. Remember that it's by fixing such little things that a report is improved.

Arranging Details

A Word About Craft

Before you are finished with school, you will have to write a number of reports and essays. One of the ways to make them more interesting for your reader is to make sure you arrange the details of your report in the best possible order. In the writing model that I included in this section of the guide, I have arranged the details in chronological order. But there are other ways to arrange details in different types of reports. You could use the following different approaches: Order the details in importance, which means that you begin with the least important details and work toward the most important. You could also start with the most important details, for greater impact at the start of your report, and work toward the less important details. For example, if I wanted to list the reason why the United States entered World War I from least important to most important, I might have written something like this: "Because it did not directly affect most Americans, the fighting among European countries was the least important reason for the United States entering World

War I. German submarine warfare was not a real concern for President Wilson until Germany declared unrestricted warfare. German diplomatic treachery wasn't much of an issue until the Zimmermann telegram showed that Germany was trying to entice Mexico to become hostile to the United States."

You could show cause and effect by describing the cause of a problem, then the effects that resulted from that problem. For example, what are the causes (or the effect) of the United States entering World War I? My sample report is a cause-and-effect report, but the causes and effects are explained as they happen — in chronological order.

Order of location, in which you arrange details in the order in which you encounter them, is yet another approach. For example, if you were describing your bedroom and you were standing at the door, you might describe the items in your bedroom as you move around the room from left to right. Or, from right to left. This sort of arrangement is most appropriately used in descriptive reports and essays. (See page 213 for how to write a descriptive essay.)

Revision Checklist

No matter how good you think your first draft is, it can be improved with careful revision. I know writers who love to revise. I'm not especially fond of rewriting, but I know how important it is, so I always try my best to revise thoughtfully. It's the only way to make a piece of writing — no matter what kind of writing — sparkle.

When you are ready to revise, it's a good thing to remember that "revision" means to see again. By that I mean to see the piece of writing in a new way, not merely to see it a second time the same way you saw it the first. When you see something anew, you will be able to notice things that need to be fixed. They may be little things — like a misspelling here or a misplaced adverb there — or they may be prominent things that could significantly affect your report. I'm talking about things like leaving out important facts or having events in the wrong order. Revising attentively is the only way to catch and correct such mistakes.

If you have a writing partner in your class, you're lucky, because a good writing partner who can read your report and offer helpful feedback can help you improve your writing. (Don't forget that you can be a good writing partner to someone else in your class.) You are especially lucky if your partner doesn't know as much as you do about the subject of your report. Why is that? Because she will be able to see the paper with fresh eyes. In other words, she will ask the questions that you need to make sure your report answers. Chances are your audience will know as little about your topic as your partner, so you'll want to make sure that you have those questions answered in your report.

The whole point of revising is to look for things that you can change to make your report stronger. One of the things that I have, on occasion, found difficult to do is take out something in a draft, feeling, I suppose, that everything in the draft is "too good" to cut. Of course, that's simply not true. Nothing in a report is too good to cut if it doesn't make your report clearer. So, when you revise, be ready to take out things that don't help make the report clear and precise. On the other hand, you may need to add some details to make your report more complete. You may also need to reorganize some parts. Some phrases and sentences may need to be rewritten. It's all part of revising your writing, a crucial part of the writing process if you want your writing to be as good as it can be.

So, after you have completed the draft of your report, put it out of sight for a few days. Give yourself some time away from it. Then, when you read it again, you will be more likely to see it in a new way. As you begin to revise your paper, look for things that you can cut, add, rewrite, or reorganize. Those things may be in the content or in the style of the report. In other words, you will be checking what you've included in your report as well as the way it's written.

Let me mention some general things to keep in mind as you revise and rewrite. As I explain how to write other types of reports and essays

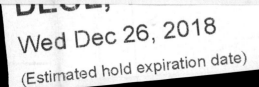

in this guide, I will remind you of som
areas of revising to consider that are

What can you add to your

→ Look for details and facts — like
   the main idea in each paragr
   details to support each topic s

→ Do you have transitional words
   to paragraph smooth?

→ Does each paragraph have a t
   plete, or do you stop before
   next point too soon?

What can you cut from

→ Do you repeat yourself? Pe
   use the same phrase too of
   to your topic? Do you inclu
   boring.) Do you just say t
   report?

→ Do all your sentences mak
   make a point?

→ Do you repeat the same
   look for suitable synonyn

What can you reorg

→ Do all your sentences
   rearrange the words and
   your report have a beg
   parts that you can switc
   report. Do your parag
   end? Sometimes, swit

As you revise and rewrite, remember that finding things in your report that need to be fixed is not a sign that you're a bad writer. It means that there are sections of your writing that need your attention. And, it means that you are careful enough to notice such problems. Congratulate yourself for that. So, fix what needs to be fixed in your report and try to be on the lookout for the same problem the next time you have a report to write. For example, if you notice that you have a problem with run-on sentences — too many ideas jammed into a single sentence — watch your sentences more carefully when you draft your next report.

Finishing Touches

Before you hand in your report to your teacher, you need to include a few pieces that will make your report complete: a cover page, which is the very first page of the report; an outline, which comes after the cover page and before the report itself; and a bibliography, a list of all the sources where you found your information, which is the very last part of the report.

The cover page and the outline are pretty self-explanatory. You can easily follow the examples that I have included in my writing model. Just remember that each Roman numeral in the outline is a main idea for a paragraph, and the parts that follow it are the facts and information that support the main idea of each paragraph.

The bibliography, however, needs careful attention because all the information in the bibliography must be in a specific order with specific punctuation marks in the right places. Remember that a bibliography is a list of the books and magazines and other sources that you used for your report. All your sources are listed alphabetically by the author's last name or, if there is no author, by the title of the book or article. When your entry goes to more than one line, the lines after the first line are indented, just like at the beginning of a paragraph. Here are some examples of the most common sources you will be likely to use:

Books

Single Author

Author's name (last name first). Title of the book (book titles are italicized or underlined). City where the book was published: publisher, copyright year (the copyright year is found on the first page or two of the book).

Morison, Samuel Eliot. *A History of the American People*. New York: Oxford University Press, 1965.

Two Authors

A book with two authors will follow the same pattern as a book by a single author, with the exception of how the authors are listed:

Hoobler, Dorothy, and Thomas Hoobler. *The Trenches: Fighting on the Western Front in World War I*. New York: Putnam Books, Inc., 1978.

Magazines

Author's name (last name first). Title of the article (article titles are enclosed in quotation marks). Name of the magazine (like the title of a book, each word is in italics or underlined separately). Volume number, date (include day, month, year, or whatever information applies. A monthly magazine, for example, would not have a day of issue, only a month and a year): page numbers of the article.

O'Brien, P. K. "The Economic Effects of the Great War." *History Today*. Vol. 44, December 1994: 22–9.

Newspapers

Author's name (last name first). Title of the article (newspaper-article titles are in quotation marks). Name of the newspaper (like the title of a book or magazine, each word is in italics or underlined separately). Date of publication, section and page number.

Johnson, Fred. "America Enters War!" *The Portland Press-Herald*. Nov. 15, 1916, A 1.

Encyclopedias

Author's name (last name first, if available). Article title (encyclopedia-article titles are enclosed in quotation marks). Title of the reference book (each word in italics or underlined). Edition. Date published, volume number, page number(s) of entire article.

"Lusitania." *Encyclopedia Americana*. International Edition. 1994, Vol. 17, p. 858.

Videotapes or Film

Title of videotape or film (videotape and film titles are italicized or each word is underlined separately). Medium (film, videotape, etc.). Production company, date. Time length.

All Quiet on the Western Front. Videotape. Norman Rosemont Productions, 1979. 150 min.

Internet

Since the source information given on the Internet is not yet uniform, you need to include as much of it as you can. Enclose the Internet address in < >. I recommend you print out any information you get online, because the Internet site information will be printed on the bottom of the page, which will allow you to easily find that site again if you need to.

Author's name (last name first, if given). Title of article (Internet-article titles are enclosed in quotation marks). Internet: <address>. Date you found the information.

Johnson, Fred. "The Entry of the United States into World War I." Internet: <www.worldwarone.edu>. January 1, 2003.

Computer Software (CD-ROMs, Disks, Etc.)

Author's name (last name first, if given). Title of software. Computer software. Name of publisher, copyright date or date of publication. Type of software (CD-ROM, disk, etc.).

Johnson, Fred. *The United States in Time of War*. Computer software. ABC Educational Technologies, 1999. CD-ROM.

The Final Copy

If you give yourself enough time to write the report without rushing, you can now put your revised report away and not look at it for a day or two.

Give your mind a short vacation from the report. After a couple of days, read the report aloud with pencil in hand, keeping a sharp eye and ear alerted to anything in the final report that needs to be fixed. Chances are you'll find a few things that can still be improved. Once you make those last changes, you are ready to print out your final copy and hand it in to your teacher.

WHY THE UNITED STATES ENTERED WORLD WAR I

by Paul B. Janeczko

Social Studies

Ms. Perez

January 1, 2003

OUTLINE

I. Introduction.

II. World War I spreads quickly across Europe.

    A. Causes of the war in Europe.

    B. The assassination of Archduke Franz Ferdinand.

    C. Battle lines quickly drawn.

    D. Wilson keeps the U.S. out of the war.

    E. Events change that.

III. Early German warfare angers many in the U.S.

    A. England blockades Germany.

    B. Germany creates war zone for subs.

    C. Germany sinks several ships; some U.S. deaths.

    D. *Lusitania* sinks, killing 128 Americans.

   E. Germany pays damages for losses.

   F. Germany stops sinking unarmed ships.

IV. Germany changes its submarine policies.

   A. Germany resumes "unrestricted submarine warfare."

   B. Wilson breaks diplomatic ties with Germany.

   C. Many Americans want war.

   D. Wilson resists.

 V. Zimmermann telegram involves Mexico.

   A. Telegram intercepted and deciphered by British.

   B. Germany plans to ask Mexico to fight U.S.

   C. Germany returns New Mexico, Arizona, Texas to Mexico.

VI. Zimmermann telegram is made public.

   A. At first British hold on to telegram.

   B. Wilson breaks ties with Germany.

   C. British send telegram to Wilson.

   D. Wilson is outraged.

   E. Wilson makes telegram public

   F. Congress declares war on Germany on April 6, 1917.

   G. Congress declares war on Austria-Hungary eight months later.

VII. Conclusion.

WHY THE UNITED STATES ENTERED WORLD WAR I
by Paul B. Janeczko

Everybody knows that World War I was the first war of the twentieth century. It involved many European nations, as well as Russia. The United States did not enter the war until it had been raging for a few years. Why would our country enter a war that was being fought on the other side of the Atlantic? As you might imagine, the answer to that question is not a simple one.

World War I started in 1914, following the assassination of Archduke Franz Ferdinand of Austria. However, the war had been brewing for a long time in Europe. Four factors contributed to the conflict: "a rise of nationalism, a buildup of military might, competition for colonies, and a system of military alliances" (*World Book*, 452).

In light of these problems, it didn't take long before the battle lines were drawn, Germany, Austria-Hungary, and Italy on one side, and Great Britain, France, and Russia on the other. As the war dragged on, President Wilson managed to keep the United States out of it (*Grolier*). In fact, when Wilson was elected for a second term in 1916, his campaign slogan boasted, "He kept us out of war" (Stokesbury, 221). However, several key events that took place during the war left Wilson with no choice but to commit the United States to what became known as the Great War.

One of the reasons the United States entered the war was German submarine warfare. When England blockaded German ports in 1915, Germany declared a "war zone" around England and warned all nations to steer clear of this area (*Grolier*). A few ships were sunk, and a few American lives were lost. But Americans were stunned when the British ship *Lusitania* was torpedoed and sunk off the coast of Ireland on May 7. Nearly 1,100 people were killed, including 128 Americans (Morison, 852). The president protested to Germany against this act, and Germany agreed to pay some of the monetary damages for the loss of property and lives. It also agreed to stop sinking unarmed ships (*Grolier*).

Things changed at the start of 1917, when Germany announced it would resume "unrestricted submarine warfare." Wilson "had no choice except to sever diplomatic relations" (*Americana*, 335) with Germany, which he did on February 3, 1917. More and more Americans were calling for Wilson to declare war. He resisted. But not for long.

In February, the British intercepted and deciphered a telegram from Arthur Zimmermann, the German foreign minister, to the German minister in Mexico. The telegram was asking Mexico to enter the war on

Germany's side. If Mexico did, the United States would be so involved with fighting on its southern border, that it would not be able to enter the war on the side of the British (*American Heritage*, 203). The so-called Zimmermann telegram offered Mexico "generous financial support and it is understood that Mexico is to re-conquer the lost territory in New Mexico, Texas, and Arizona" (Hicks, 404).

Admiral Sir William R. Hall, the head of British code-breakers, decided to hang on to this "juicy bit of stupidity until the time was right" (Stokesbury, 221). He didn't have to wait long. When Wilson cut off relations with Germany, Hall delivered the Zimmermann telegram to the president. Needless to say, Wilson was shocked by Germany's plan. On March 1, the Zimmermann telegram "made headlines all over the U.S." (Stokesbury, 221). A month later, on April 6, 1917, Congress declared war on Germany. By the end of the year, it declared war on Austria-Hungary.

Although President Wilson was able to keep the United States out of the Great War for several years, the actions of Germany made it impossible for the United States to remain neutral. Germany's unrestricted submarine warfare and its plan to involve Mexico in the war proved more than the president and Congress could stand. The United States went to war in Europe.

BIBLIOGRAPHY

1999 Grolier Multimedia Encyclopedia. Grolier
Interactive Inc., 1998. CD-ROM.

The American Heritage Book of World War I, editors
of *American Heritage* magazine. New York: Simon
& Schuster, 1964.

Hicks, John D., George E. Mowry, and Robert E.
Burke. *The American Nation.* Boston: Houghton Mifflin
Co., 1963.

Morison, Samuel Eliot. *A History of the American People.*
New York: Oxford University Press, 1965.

Stokesbury, James L. *A Short History of World War I.*
New York: William Morris & Co., 1981.

"World War I," *Encyclopedia Americana,* 1998, Vol. 29,
pp. 216–363.

"World War I," *The World Book Encyclopedia,* 2001, Vol.
21, pp. 452–467.

CHAPTER THREE

Writing a Social Studies Report

in 1969 as the brainchild
vanted to open a recordi
illage in upstate New Yo
Bob Dylan. The businessm
attract a lot of attention
ometown. Although they h
s to risk money on t
vestors were interested
of this project that was
Music and Art Fo
Days of Peace a
accommodate
end the fair, t

e was move
nsidered wh
bassing any "m
lence" (American
peace singers like A
her acts were soon
rformers read like a
luding the Grateful
arwater Revival, and
o took pains to plan f
ilities, and a medical st
t went into Woodstoc

f you've read the previous chapter, you should have a good sense of how to research and write a quality report, regardless of the subject. But if your social studies teacher walks into the room and tells you that the topic of your social studies report is totally up to you, what do you do? Panic? Maybe, but I hope not for long. With some thinking and planning, you can come up with a social studies topic that will be perfect for your report.

Getting Ideas

You may be one of those students who knows immediately what you're going to write your social studies report about. You might be fascinated by the American Civil War and know that you will write about some aspect of that war. Or you may be interested in how the American government confined thousands of Japanese to internment camps during World War II. If you have a social studies topic that works for you, get started on the research as soon as you can, although you should check with your teacher to make sure your topic is acceptable for the assignment.

If, on the other hand, you don't have a clue what to write your social studies report about, I suggest you start by thinking of American history as a series of decades. Each decade has events, characters, and themes that set it apart from other decades. How can you find out what happened during those decades? Go to the library and look for a book that breaks down American history into decades. *The Timetables of History*, by Bernard Grum, is one good source. Another is the Time-Life series, The Fabulous Century, which gives a full volume to each decade of the twentieth century. Or, you could do what I did. I went to www.google.com and typed in "American history time line" and came up with some very helpful Web sites:

➜ www.historytimeline.com

➜ guweb2.gonzaga.edu/faculty/campbell/enl311/timeframe

➜ www.si.edu/resource/faq/nmah/timeline

➡ americanhistory.si.edu/timeline/index

When I looked at these Web sites, I found a few possible starting points for my social studies report:

➡ 1920s: Al Capone, Presidents Harding and Coolidge, the *Scopes* "monkey" trial, women get the right to vote, the Harlem Renaissance

➡ 1930s: Presidents Hoover and Roosevelt, the Great Depression, the Dust Bowl, Anne Frank, the *Scottsboro* trial

➡ 1940s: World War II, the D-Day invasion, the Holocaust, the atomic bomb, the end of the war

➡ 1950s: Golden Age of Television, the Korean War, President Eisenhower, fads and fashion, Joseph Stalin, Joseph McCarthy

➡ 1960s: the psychedelic '60s, President Nixon, the Vietnam War, war protests, the Cold War

Even though you may not know anything about some of the items on the list, you may find things that interest you enough to explore further. Maybe you read Karen Hesse's book *Out of the Dust* and you'd like to find out more about the Dust Bowl. Or, if you're into science, you might want to looking into the *Scopes* "monkey" trial, since the notion of the evolution of man was at the center of the trial. If you're a TV nut, you might want to see how that box was actually invented and turned into a fixture in homes all over the world. By breaking the century into decades and checking the time lines, you may surprise yourself by discovering a topic for your social studies report.

Getting Organized

As you look for a topic, remember that you shouldn't try to write a report on the 1960s, for example. There is simply too much that must be part of a report that covers an entire decade. Since the '60s interests me, I decided that I wanted to find one small part of that time period that could work for me in a short report.

What aspects of the '60s might I write about? To find that out, I created a web that looked like what appears below:

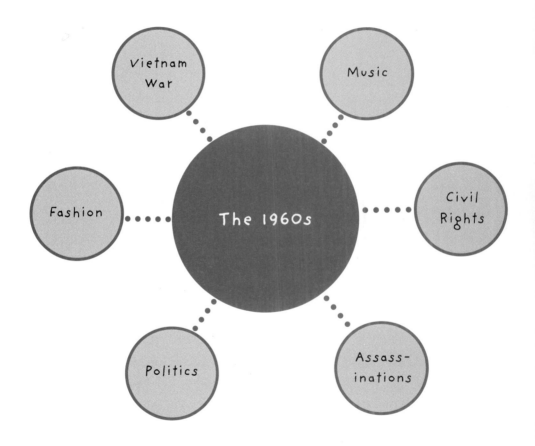

I found that most of these aspects of that decade interest me, but I decided that I would zero in on the music. This led me to create another web with music at the center:

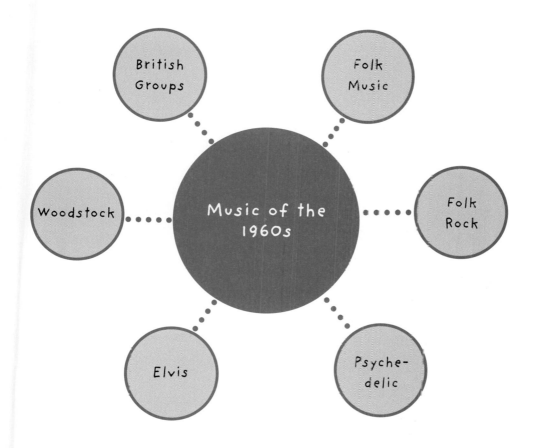

After completing the web, I decided that I would write my sample social studies report about Woodstock, the music festival that occurred in the summer of 1969. It seemed to be a subject that I could handle in three or four pages.

First-Person Accounts

Research Tip

When I researched Woodstock for my sample social studies report, one of the things that I quickly discovered was that there were quite a few first-person accounts of the music festival. In other words, reports by people who actually attended Woodstock. Some of their reports appeared in magazines and counterculture newspapers. Other accounts were part of oral history projects that had been transcribed and gathered in books. Reading these first-person accounts actually gave me the feeling of being a member of the throng that made history on that August weekend over thirty years ago.

One of the advantages of writing your report about something that occurred in this century — especially in, say, the past fifty years — is that you can very likely get some eyewitness accounts of the event. Or, if you are writing about a theme, like the early days of television, you can find some accounts by people who were part of that process. Finally, don't overlook someone who was part of history. You might have a neighbor who was part of a civil rights march in the early '60s. Or maybe you have a grandfather who stormed the beach at Normandy or survived the Dust Bowl. People who participated in history are legitimate sources of information.

Writing the Draft

As I did research on Woodstock, it became clear to me that my notes seemed to fall into a chronological order. I had notes on how the idea of Woodstock came about, how the planning started, why things started going wrong, which musicians were booked, and what actually happened there. So, I decided that I'd write my report as a chronological narrative.

Having decided that, I needed to keep my story line in mind as I wrote my report. What happened first. What happened next. And so on, until I finished telling the story. So, as I wrote my draft I double-checked my notes to make sure I was putting events in the right order. Although I knew my social studies report was going to be short, I wanted to make sure that my readers got a clear picture of what happened at Woodstock.

Revision Checklist

➡ Do I have enough good information to tell my story? Are there any information gaps that I need to fill?

➡ Will my reader be able to follow the sequence of events that I present in my report?

➡ Have I included appropriate transitional words to get me from one part of the story to the next?

➡ Does my introduction make the reader want to continue reading my report?

➡ Do I have a satisfying conclusion that smoothly ends my report?

THREE DAYS OF PEACE AND MUSIC:

THE STORY OF WOODSTOCK

by Paul B. Janeczko

Social Studies

Ms. Perez

January 1, 2003

OUTLINE

I. Introduction.

II. The idea started as a brainchild of two businessmen.

    A. They intended to open a recording studio.

    B. Investors were unwilling to risk money for the studio.

    C. They were willing to invest in Woodstock Music and Art Fair.

III. The planning began.

    A. No proviolence acts were invited.

    B. Big-name acts agreed to participate.

    C. Provisions were made for security, food, first aid, and sanitation.

IV. Things started to go wrong immediately.

    A. Promoters couldn't get a permit in Wallkill.

    B. The site of fair was moved to Bethel.

    C. The name of Woodstock was retained.

V. Woodstock was a victim of its own success.

    A. Nearly 500,000 attended.

    B. Fans broke down gates.

    C. Woodstock became a free event.

    D. Massive traffic jams kept performers and fans
       away.

VI. Other problems developed.

    A. The hot dog trailer lost refrigeration.

    B. The revolving stage didn't work.

    C. There were not enough working toilets.

    D. Rain turned the pasture muddy.

VI. Woodstock became a legend.

    A. It was "three days of peace and music."

    B. There was no violence.

    C. A strong sense of community developed.

VII. Conclusion.

· ·

THREE DAYS OF PEACE AND MUSIC:
THE STORY OF WOODSTOCK
by Paul B. Janeczko

What do you call a gathering of half a million rain-
drenched people who come to a pasture in upstate New
York to listen to rock and roll? Woodstock. Because
from August 15 to 17, 1969, that's exactly what
happened. What started out as a music-and-art fair
became a legendary chapter in the history of rock and
roll. But it almost didn't happen at all.

The idea started in 1969 as the brainchild of two businessmen. They wanted to open a recording studio in Woodstock, a village in upstate New York that was the home of Bob Dylan. The businessmen thought their studio would attract a lot of attention if they built it in Dylan's hometown. Although they had trouble getting investors to risk money on the recording studio, two investors were interested in financing another aspect of this project that was to be known as the Woodstock Music and Art Fair (*American History*, 46).

Planning began for what was advertised as "Three Days of Peace and Music." Because Woodstock could not accommodate all the fans that were expected to attend the fair, the site was moved to nearby Wallkill. The organizers considered which artists to invite to perform, bypassing any "music groups and speakers advocating violence" (*American History*, 47) and featuring propeace singers like Arlo Guthrie and Joan Baez. Other acts were soon added, until the list of performers read like a who's who of rock and roll, including the Grateful Dead, The Band, Creedence Clearwater Revival, and Janis Joplin. The promoters also took pains to plan for security, food, sanitation facilities, and a medical staff.

Despite all the planning that went into Woodstock, "the festival began to go wrong almost immediately" (Britannica.com). For one thing, the village of Wallkill wouldn't give the promoters a permit to stage their fair. Consequently, it was moved to a 600-acre farm in Bethel, New York, about fifty miles from Woodstock. Despite the change in location, promoters kept the name of Woodstock (Echoes.com).

In some ways Woodstock was a victim of its own success. The promoters were expecting that about 200,000 people would spend eighteen dollars each for a three-day ticket to the music-and-arts activities. As it turned out, nearly half a million people arrived at Woodstock — or tried to arrive. As the crowds began to surge through the gates, promoters realized that there was no way they were going to get any admission fees from the crowd, so the fair became a free event (Weiser). The huge crowd led to massive traffic jams in the area near Bethel, but also on the New York Thruway, a major highway to the area. Some people rode on the hoods of the crawling cars and bantered back and forth. "Tons of supplies, and even some musicians were stuck in the traffic jams and never made it to the site" (Weiser).

Some of the problems at Woodstock had nothing to do with the traffic. The revolving stage "designed to eliminate intermissions between acts was the biggest and the most expensive ever built." However, once the music equipment was loaded on the stage, it would revolve an inch (*Popular Culture*, 177). Another problem caused by the overflowing crowd was the lack of working toilets. To make matters worse, hot dogs in a forty-foot trailer rotted when the refrigeration fuel ran out, and "thousands of people endured the stench of rancid food while they went hungry" (*Popular Culture*, 177). Then the rains came, turning the pasture into acres of mud. But that didn't stop the fun. In fact, it seemed to give people another chance to enjoy one another. As one observer put it. "There was mud everywhere. People were sliding around in it laughing" (Weiser).

Even though things went wrong and the music was not always of the best quality — Roger Daltry of The Who called their performance "the worst gig we have ever played" (Echoes.com) — Woodstock became a legend because of the sense of community that the people experienced in that muddy pasture. For many of them "the community aspect was more important than the music" (Echoes.com) as they dealt with "hunger, rain, mud, and unserviced toilets conspired to create an adversity against which people could unite and bond" (Echoes.com). As one man said, "The camp was always beautifully together, though. At night, it looked like a huge band of medieval gypsies strolling and visiting and finally doing their thing. . . . We were all in the same family" (Hilgerdt).

Despite all that went wrong at Woodstock, it turned out to be "three days of peace and music." Although news media predicted riots from so many unruly young people, violence "never erupted" — not even a fistfight — despite food shortages, an overwhelmed medical staff, and inadequate toilet facilities (*ABC-CLIO,* 337). Three people were born and two died, just about what you would expect in a city of nearly 500,000 people. As one observer noted, "Woodstock was a mastermind idea that occurred at just the right time" (Echoes.com).

BIBLIOGRAPHY

Graves, Tom. "Peace, Love, Music." *American History.* Vol. 6, Issue 30, Jan.-Feb. 1996: 47-48.

Hamilton, Neil A. *The ABC-CLIO Companion to the 1960s Counterculture in America.* Santa Barbara, CA: ABC-CLIO, Inc., 1997.

Hilgerdt, Jack. "That Aquarian Exposition: We Are One." http://www.celticguitarmusic.com. January 25, 2002.

Layman, Richard, ed. *American Decades: 1960-1969.* Detroit: Gale Research, 1995.

Weiser, Glenn. "Woodstock '69 Remembered." http://www.celticguitarmusic.com. January 25, 2002.

"Woodstock." http://www.britannica.com. January 25, 2002.

"Woodstock." http://www.echoes.com. January 25, 2002.

"Woodstock." *The St. James Encyclopedia of Popular Culture.* Vol. 5. Detroit: The St. James Press, 2000.

CHAPTER FOUR

Writing About a Person in History

in 1969 as the brainchild
wanted to open a recordi
illage in upstate New Yo
Bob Dylan. The businessm
attract a lot of attention
ometown. Although they h
s to risk money on t
vestors were interested
of this projec that was
Music and Art F
Days of Peace a
t accommodate
end the fair, t
e was move
nsidered wh
assing any "m
lence" (American
peace singers like A
er acts were soon
rformers read like a
luding the Grateful
arwater Revival, and
o took pains to plan f
ilities, and a medical st
t went into Woodstoc

Because so many of the subjects you study in school involve people, the chances are quite good that somewhere along the line, you're going to have to write a report about a person. Perhaps you'll be required to write a report about a scientist or a politician. Or about a writer or an inventor. As far as your research is concerned, it doesn't make much difference what kind of person you will be writing about. The research process will be basically the same as the one I outlined in the basic report chapter (starting on page 17).

Getting Ideas

Try to pick someone who interests you. If the person doesn't interest you, it's going to be tough for you to write a report that interests someone else. While almost all students prefer to write a report on a topic of their own choosing, that is not always possible. Imagine this scenario: You walk into a class one day and your teacher announces in a cheerful voice, "I have compiled a list of topics for your research reports. I would like each of you to write a report on a famous American. I will assign each of you the name of the person about whom you must write your report."

When the teacher works her way to your name on the class list, she tells you that you must write about Rosa Parks. You blink. Who is Rosa Parks? you ask yourself. You may have only a hazy recollection that she was involved in the civil rights movement, but you're really not sure who she is. Asking that question — who is she? — is a good way to start your report because it's the question you must answer in your report.

Since you know little about Rosa Parks except that your teacher has told you that she is a famous American, you need to begin your search by going to an encyclopedia, that treasure trove of general information. (See "Research Tip: A Few Words About Encyclopedias" on page 27.) Your library probably has several different sets of encyclopedias, but since Rosa Parks is an American, your best bet is to look at the *Encyclopedia Americana* first.

You find the *P* volume and turn to her entry. After reading that she is an African-American civil rights activist, you find the real answer to your question in the very first paragraph of the article on Rosa Parks: Her refusal to surrender her bus seat to a white man and subsequent arrest ignited the Montgomery, Alabama, bus boycott of 1955–1956, and is regarded as the beginning of the modern U.S. civil rights movement.

The information in that sentence is like a series of road signs pointing you to different places to do your research. Take time to consider where those road signs will send you: First of all, because you will be reporting on a person's life, you will want to consult an encyclopedia that specializes in biographical information. You also know that she is an African American woman, which should give you reason to look in books that feature biographies of women and biographies of African-Americans. Finally, because you know that she was involved in the early days of the American civil rights movement, you might also want to investigate some books on that subject.

Biographical Reference Books

Research Tip

While an encyclopedia like *Encyclopedia Britannica* or *The World Book Encyclopedia* is a great place to find general information, you cannot limit yourself to those books when you find yourself with research to do about a person. There are a number of excellent reference books that deal with the lives and accomplishments of famous people. Some may be in the reference area of your school library; others will be available in larger public libraries.

African-American Biography
Biography Index
Chambers Biographical Dictionary
Contemporary Authors
Current Biography Yearbook
Dictionary of American Biography

Dictionary of Scientific Biography
Merriam-Webster's Biographical Dictionary
The McGraw-Hill Encyclopedia of World Biography
Notable American Women 1607-1950
UXL Encyclopedia of Native American Tribes
Who Was When?: A Dictionary of Contemporaries
World Authors

While these biographical encyclopedias will give you lots of worthwhile information, always be on the lookout for other features that might help you. Many of the articles in these books will list some other sources of information on a subject. They may, for instance, suggest some books or magazine articles that you could read.

Taking Notes

Although you'll be working with some specialized reference books, you want to start your note-taking by getting some general information about your subject, Rosa Parks. You decide to first check *The Encyclopedia of World Biography*, a multivolume set that includes information about famous people from around the world. In Volume 12 you find a long article on Rosa Parks, so you write out your first source card. You remember to put that all-important source number in the upper right-hand corner of the card.

> Rosa Parks   [#1]
>
> *The Encyclopedia of World Biography*
>
> Detroit: Gale Research, 1989

With your resource safely noted on a card, you're ready to take notes. Remember to put the notes in your own words and to make sure you mark each card with your resource number as well as the number of the page on which you found the information. And, to make organizing your notes easier, you need to write a category heading at the top of each note.

Early childhood   [#1, p. 115]

-Born Feb. 4, 1913, as Rosa McCauley

-Tuskegee, AL.

-Mother: teacher; father: carpenter

Schooling   [#1, p. 115]

-Montgomery Industrial School for Girls

-Graduates 1928: Booker T. Washington H.S. (all-
    African-American school)

-Attends Alabama State College for a short time

Early adult life   [#1, p. 115]

-Marries Raymond Parks, barber, 1932

-Both active in civil rights causes

-Member: NAACP youth council

-1943 voted secretary of NAACP Montgomery branch

-Various jobs: housekeeper, insurance salesperson,
    seamstress

Later life   [#1, p. 115]

-Moves to Detroit, 1957

-Hard to find work

-Finds work for U.S. Representative John Conyers

Awards   [#1, p. 115]

-1979: NAACP Spingarn Medal

-Freedom Award from Southern Christian Leadership
  Conference (SCLC)

-1980: Martin Luther King, Jr., Nonviolent Peace Prize

-1984: Eleanor Roosevelt Women of Courage Award

-1988: founded Rosa & Raymond Parks Institute for
  Self-Development, to train black youths

-1989: becomes president of Institute

-"Virtually no history of the modern civil rights movement
  in the U.S. fails to mention the role of Rosa Parks."

Except for the very last note, which is a direct quotation from this source, everything is in your own words. You decide to include the final quotation because it makes a very important point about Rosa Parks. It's the kind of quotation that would work very well in your introduction or in your conclusion.

When you finish the entry in *The Encyclopedia of World Biography*, you turn to *The Biographical Dictionary of Black Americans*, a reference book with a more specific focus. However, since you've already gotten such good information, you take only a few notes from this source.

Rosa Parks [#2]

The Biographical Dictionary of Black Americans

Rachel Kranz

New York: Facts on File, 1992

Early adult life [#2, p. 114]

-Civil rights work is voluntary and not-for-profit, so she
takes up sewing

Later life [#2, p. 115]

-Joins her brother in Detroit

-Homeless for a while

-She and her husband suffer severe health problems

-Continues to raise money for NAACP

Next, you consult *Current Biography Yearbook* by looking up Rosa Parks in the index. Since you already have some good notes, you don't find much in this reference book. The same can be said for the other sources you consult.

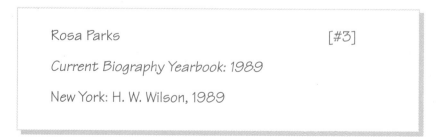

Rosa Parks [#3]

Current Biography Yearbook: 1989

New York: H. W. Wilson, 1989

Later life [#3, p. 431]

-1965: goes to work for Conyers

-Wants to be remembered as a person who wanted to be
  free and wanted others to be free

The Civil Rights Movement [#4]

Sanford Wexler

New York: Facts on File, 1993

Observations [#4, p. 321]

-Jesse Jackson calls her the mother of the civil rights
  movement

Rosa Parks [#5]

The World Book Encyclopedia

Chicago: World Book Inc., 1999

Awards [#5, p. 172]

-1999: Congressional Gold Medal

-1992: writes *Rosa Parks: My Story*

The last source you consult is a short autobiographical book by Rosa Parks herself. You are looking for a good quotation to include in your report. You find exactly what you are looking for.

> Quiet Strength   [#6]
>
> Rosa Parks
>
> Grand Rapids, MI: Zondervan Publishing, 1994

> [#6, p. 25]
>
> -"My feet were not tired, but I was tired — tired of unfair treatment."

Getting Organized

Since you'll be telling the story of a person's life in this report, a good way to organize your notes is to draw a time line of the person's life, and as you read over your notes, mark the important events on the time line. This will give you the opportunity to read over your notes and put the events in chronological order. More important than that, it will make writing the outline for this report easier.

Give yourself lots of space for your time line. A two-page spread in your writer's notebook sounds about right to me. At the start of your time line, you will write the year in which the person was born. At the end will be the year in which the person died. If the person is still alive, then you can use the current year as the final date on your time line.

Once you have your time line drawn and the beginning and ending dates written down, you are ready to read carefully through your notes, filling in the important events and dates in a person's life along that time line. My time line for Rosa Parks looked like this:

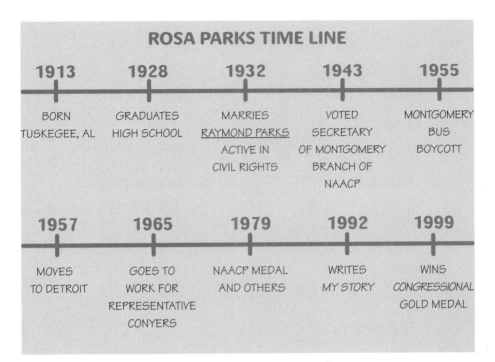

ROSA PARKS TIME LINE

1913	1928	1932	1943	1955
BORN TUSKEGEE, AL	GRADUATES HIGH SCHOOL	MARRIES RAYMOND PARKS ACTIVE IN CIVIL RIGHTS	VOTED SECRETARY OF MONTGOMERY BRANCH OF NAACP	MONTGOMERY BUS BOYCOTT

1957	1965	1979	1992	1999
MOVES TO DETROIT	GOES TO WORK FOR REPRESENTATIVE CONYERS	NAACP MEDAL AND OTHERS	WRITES MY STORY	WINS CONGRESSIONAL GOLD MEDAL

When you have completed your time line, you might very well see some gaps in your story that need more research. You can fill those in by doing more research. Then you're ready to write your outline.

A Word About Craft

Writing a Topic Outline

After you've written down all your notes and organized the cards according to the topics written at the top of each card, take a look at the time line you've constructed. You should see a logical way to organize your report — chronological order — and put that order into a simple topic outline. You will notice that the topic outline is different from the sentence outline that I wrote in the basic-report section of this guide. In some cases, you'll find that a topic outline works better than a full-sentence outline. In this case, for example, simply writing "Childhood" works better than something like "Rosa Parks's childhood in the

South," which adds nothing to the outline. If, however, there is a common thread to her childhood (as well as to other main parts of your report), then you might want to use a sentence outline. For example, if you write something like "Rosa Parks's childhood was marked by tragedy," then you might want to use a sentence outline. But for this report, the topic outline works fine:

I. Introduction

II. Childhood

III. Early adult life

IV. Confrontation on the bus

V. The bus boycott

VI. After the boycott

VII. Conclusion

Happy with this brief topic outline, you expand it by adding more details from your notes. When you do that, you come up with this outline:

I. Introduction

II. Childhood

    A. Born in Tuskegee, Alabama, February 4, 1913

    B. Moves to Montgomery

    C. Attends Montgomery Industrial School

    D. Graduates from Booker T. Washington H.S.

III. Early adult life

    A. Marries Ray Parker, 1932

    B. Works for civil rights causes

    C. Member NAACP

    D. Secretary of NAACP Montgomery branch

    E. Holds several jobs

   IV. Confrontation on the bus
        A. Takes seat in black section
        B. Is asked to move when more whites get on bus
        C. Rosa Parks refuses
        D. Police arrive and arrest her
    V. The bus boycott
        A. Montgomery Improvement Association sues
           city
        B. Boycott continues while case is tried
        C. Supreme Court rules segregation laws
           unconstitutional
        D. Boycott ends after 382 days
   VI. Later life
        A. Unable to find work
        B. Moves to Detroit
        C. Rosa and husband have health problems
        D. Continues to work for civil rights
        E. Begins work for U.S. Congressman John
           Conyers
 VII. Conclusion

Writing the Draft

The most logical way to write about a person's life is to tell her story in chronological order, the same order in which we all live our lives. And the same way you wrote your time line for the subject's life. There may be one turning-point event in a person's life that you want to feature in your report, like the Montgomery bus boycott in the life of Rosa Parks. Or there may be several noteworthy events over the course of a person's life that you will describe in your report.

In general, you will want to keep in mind the stages that a person's life passes through: birth, childhood, adolescence, early adult life, middle age, old age, death. Chances are that you will not give each stage in a person's life the same emphasis because, inevitably, some stages of her life will be more important than others.

This brings me to an important two-sided question about writing in general, but writing about a person's life in particular. What do you include? What do you leave out? The easiest way to answer these questions is to suggest that you include as much as possible. The danger with that approach is that you run the risk of including too much, for fear that you will leave out something important. And that's a natural worry, especially for a beginning writer. But you must learn to trust your own sense of what is important enough to include in your report and what can safely be left out. Remember that you are writing a short report and not a book about the person.

Let me share a writer's trick with you. After I have researched a subject, I read over my notes very carefully. As I read them, I jot down the ten most important things I learned in my research. I use that list as a guide to what should be in the article, because chances are people who read my article will find those points important, too. My list is written on a sheet of paper and not engraved in stone, so I am free to change the list as I write the article. And that's what usually happens as I develop the piece. But that's okay. As a writer, you need to be flexible and willing to make changes for the better as you work your way through the writing process.

My report on Rosa Parks (page 94) is arranged in chronological order. You will notice that I spent two paragraphs in the middle of the report talking about the Montgomery bus boycott because that was such a pivotal event in her life as well as a turning point in the history of the civil rights movement in our country. As I was writing the report, there was no doubt in my mind that I couldn't shortchange that event of her life.

With your outline complete, you're ready to work on the draft of your paper, remembering that the more work you put into making the draft complete, the easier it will be to write the final paper. This means that, even though it is a draft, you want to write it as well as you can and make it as complete as you can, thereby minimizing the corrections that you'll need to make later. It also means that you'll want to include in parentheses in the draft the sources of all your information.

It's a good idea to write the draft with your outline at hand. As you write your draft, you can check it against the outline, making sure that your report is an accurate summary of a life. You should also be certain that you're putting the stages of the person's life in the proper order.

After you have written your first draft, try to put it aside for a day or two. Try not to think about it. Then, when you do look at it again, you may be able to see the paper in a new way. Read through it carefully, marking the spots that need more work. Make any changes that you think are necessary. This would be a good time to give your paper to a writing partner and get her opinion of the report. If you don't have a writing partner, maybe a parent or a friend might be interested in reading the paper aloud to you. Remember, it can be a good thing to have someone read the paper who is unfamiliar with your subject. They might be in a good position to tell you when something doesn't make sense or when they can't follow the sequence of events in the life of your subject.

Revision Checklist

➡ Are the life events in the correct order?

➡ Do you need to add details to make the person's life clear to the reader?

➡ Can you spot any places where you repeated yourself? Take them out.

➡ Are your sentences clear and varied?

➡ Can you see the beginning, the middle, and the end of your report?

ROSA PARKS:

CIVIL RIGHTS PIONEER

by Paul B. Janeczko

Social Studies

Ms. Perez

January 1, 2003

OUTLINE

I. Introduction.

II. Childhood.

    A. Born in Tuskegee, AL, 2/4/13.

    B. Moves to Montgomery.

    C. Attends Montgomery Industrial School.

    D. Graduates from Booker T. Washington High School.

II. Early adult life.

    A. Marries Ray Parks, 1932.

    B. Works for civil rights causes.

    C. Member NAACP.

    D. Secretary of NAACP Montgomery branch.

    E. Holds several jobs.

III. Confrontation on the bus.

    A. Takes seat in black section.

    B. Is asked to move when more whites get on bus.

    C. Rosa Parks refuses.

    D. Police arrive and arrest her.

IV. The bus boycott.

      A. Montgomery Improvement Association sues city.

      B. Boycott continues while case is tried.

      C. Supreme Court rules segregation laws unconstitutional.

      D. Boycott ends after 382 days.

V. Later life.

      A. Unable to find work.

      B. Moves to Detroit.

      C. Rosa and husband have health problems.

      D. Continues to work for civil rights.

      E. Begins work for U.S. Congressman John Conyers.

VI. Conclusion.

- -

ROSA PARKS:

CIVIL RIGHTS PIONEER

The Reverend Jesse Jackson called Rosa Parks the mother of the civil rights movement (Wexler, 321). Many historians agree that virtually no history of the civil rights movement in the United States fails to mention her name (*World Biography*, 116). Yet, no one would be more surprised than Rosa Parks herself that she would play so important a part in an event that marked the beginning of the civil rights movement in our country (*World Book*, 117).

She was born Rosa McCauley in Tuskegee, Alabama, on February 4, 1913. Her mother was a schoolteacher, and her father was a carpenter. Even though the family moved to Montgomery, Alabama, Rosa's mother insisted that she continue her schooling. Rosa attended Montgomery Industrial School for Girls and later graduated from the all-African-American Booker T. Washington High School in 1928. Following high school, she attended Alabama State College for a short time (*World Biography*, 115).

After she left college, Rosa married Ray Parks, a barber, in 1932. Both she and her new husband were active in their support of civil rights causes, especially voter registration. Rosa was a member of the National Association for the Advancement of Colored People Youth Council (NAACP) and was elected secretary of the Montgomery branch in 1943 (*World Biography*, 115).

Since her civil rights work was voluntary and not-for-profit, Parks found several jobs to make ends meet (*Black Americans*, 114). She worked as a housekeeper, an insurance salesperson, and a seamstress. It was this last job that took her to the Montgomery Fair department store. When Rosa Parks left work and walked to the bus stop on the evening of December 1, 1995, she had no idea that her life would never be the same again (*Black Americans*, 114).

The buses in Montgomery were segregated, with the first ten rows reserved for white passengers. Blacks even had to pay their fare at the front of the bus, then get off and enter the bus from the rear door. That evening when Rosa Parks got on the bus, she took a seat in the first of the rows for black passengers. Soon, however, the white rows filled, and according to the law at the time, the bus driver asked the passengers in Rosa's row to move when another white passenger boarded the bus. Although the three other passengers in her row moved, Rosa refused, setting the stage for confrontation with the bus driver, who pulled the bus to the curb and brought two police officers back to the bus. When Rosa Parks again refused to move, she was arrested.

The arrest of Rosa Parks was the spark that led to the mass boycott of the city's buses. Martin Luther King, Jr., president of the Montgomery Improvement Association, sued the city, claiming its bus segregation was unconstitutional. While the suit was being decided in the courts, the boycott continued. On December 20, 1956, the Supreme Court decided that the bus segregation laws were, in fact, unconstitutional. Finally, after 382 days, the boycott was ended and blacks could sit wherever they wanted to on Montgomery buses.

Unable to find work, Rosa Parks moved to Detroit, to be near her brother. But times were not easy for her and her husband, who both suffered severe health problems (*Black Americans*, 115). They were even homeless for a while. Still, she continued to travel the country and raise money for the NAACP. In 1965, she went to work for U.S. Representative John Conyers as a receptionist and staff assistant, a position she held for thirty years (*Current Biography*, 431).

Rosa Parks has won many awards for her work on behalf of civil rights, including the Martin Luther King, Jr., Nonviolent Peace Prize; the Eleanor Roosevelt Women of Courage Award; and, in 1999, the Congressional Gold Medal. Despite all her awards and accomplishments, she remained modest about her role in the boycott. "I was not the only person involved in the boycott," she said. "I was just one of many who fought for freedom. And many others around me began to want to fight for their rights as well" (*Quiet Strength*, 27).

· ·

BIBLIOGRAPHY

Kranz, Rachel. *The Biographical Dictionary of Black Americans*. New York: Facts on File, 1992.

Parks, Rosa. *Quiet Strength*. Grand Rapids, MI: Zondervan Publishing House, 1994.

"Rosa Parks." *Current Biography Yearbook*: 1989. New York: H.W. Wilson, 1989.

"Rosa Parks." *Encyclopedia Americana*. 2000, Vol. 21, p. 464.

"Rosa Parks." *Encyclopedia of World Biography*. Detroit: Gale Research, 1998.

"Rosa Lee Parks." *The World Book Encyclopedia*, 1999, Vol. 15, pp. 171-172.

Wexler, Sanford. *The Civil Rights Movement*. New York: Facts on File, 1993.

CHAPTER FIVE

Writing About a Social Issue

in 1969 as the brainchild
vanted to open a recordi
illage in upstate New Yo
Bob Dylan. The businessm
attract a lot of attention
ometown. Although they h
s to risk money on t
vestors were interested
of this project that was
Music and Art F
Days of Peace a
t accommodate
nd the fair, t

e was move
nsidered wh
passing any "mu
lence" (American
peace singers like A
her acts were soon
rformers read like a
luding the Grateful
arwater Revival, and
o took pains to plan f
ilities, and a medical st
t went into Woodstoc

 f you pay attention to what's going on in the world around you, you'll
 recognize some issues that touch the lives of lots of people — like gun
control. Some of the issues might even touch your life, like wearing uniforms to school. Regardless of the issue you respond to, it has two sides.
When you write a report on a social issue, you're going to need to select
a topic that means a lot to you, but you'll need to be prepared to include
both sides of the issue in your report. Later in this guide, I will explain
how to write a persuasive essay in which you try to convince the reader
of the value of your position on an issue.

Getting Ideas

What social issues are important to you? You want to choose a subject
that is important to you because it's more fun to write about something
that you're interested in. Remember that your goal in this report is to
inform the reader about the issue and not to convince the reader about
one side of it. You can save that sort of writing for a persuasive essay, a
letter to the editor, or an editorial.

　　Look at the list below. Perhaps a subject that means a lot to you is on
this list:

➡ school prayer

➡ driving restrictions for teenagers

➡ cloning

➡ abortion

➡ censorship

➡ physician-assisted suicide

➡ affirmative action

➡ smokers' rights

➡ parental warning on CDs and music videos

If one of these issues is important to you, write it at the top of a page in your writer's notebook and quickly write down how you feel about the issue. Don't stop to think too much. Just write from your heart about the issue. On the next page, write the arguments you might hear from the other side of the issue. This is a good way to get you thinking about the other side of the issue, which, like it or not, you're going to have to include in a report about a social issue.

If none of these ideas is important to you, spend some time watching the news and reading the newspaper, searching for an issue that is important to you. Talk to your friends at school. Listen to the things that concern them. You can write down all the possibilities on a list in your notebook. After you have studied the list and found a subject that you will pursue in your report, try the notebook activity that I explained in the previous paragraph.

A Word About Craft

Showing Both Sides of an Issue

Writing about a social issue is tricky because you need to write about two sides of an issue and not just the side that you believe in. This means, of course, that you'll need to research both sides of the issue and try to summarize the best points for both sides. That's not an easy thing when you are convinced that one side of the issue is the right side. For example, if you are sick of the school shootings, it may not be easy to report fairly on the people who feel that there's no need for a background check of someone who wants to buy a pistol. Nevertheless, if you want to write a good report, you need to be fair and unbiased and give the reader a chance to make up her own mind.

Periodical Research

Research Tip

To write a good report on a social issue, you'll need to use the most up-to-date information. You could, of course, use recent books on the subject. But to be as current as you can be on the issue, you'll need to find information in newspapers and periodicals and online.

Many libraries maintain an archive of past issues of some popular magazines. However, most of your periodical research will be done at a computer terminal, where you'll find the correct database — my local library uses EBSCO Host. Type in the subject you are researching, and hit the return key. In seconds, you'll have a long list of magazines that contain the subject you are looking for.

There are a number of advantages to this software. First of all, the online magazine database will include many more magazines and journals that all but the largest of libraries could house. The second advantage is that many of the articles are available to be downloaded and printed right in the library. The third advantage of searching magazines online is that even if the database does not contain the full text of a particular magazine article, each entry is annotated, which means that it will contain a brief summary of the article and it will give you all the information you need — title, page number, publication date — to track down the article. The fourth advantage of online indexes is that you can frequently access such a system from your home computer and download and print articles without leaving the house. So, check with your school library and the local public library to see which online newspaper and magazine database they use. Also check to see if you can access this information from your home computer.

Even though you'll be researching mostly in magazines and newspapers instead of books, the process of researching and note-taking doesn't change. You still need to make sure you have a source-card for each source. You still need to read your research material and put information into your own words on note cards. You still need to make sure you write the source card number on each note card. What will be different, however, is the information you need for your source cards and the information you include in your bibliography. You should check page 56 to find out what information about the article you will need for your bibliography.

Getting Organized

Because you are reporting on two sides of an issue, you might want to use a graphic organizer similar to the one I explained at the start of this section on page 101. It will allow you to see, at a glance, the points you make for both sides of the issue. If you open your writer's notebook to a two-page spread of clean sheets, that will give you enough room for a good graphic organizer for this type of report. At the top of the left page, write "FOR" in big letters. At the top of the right page, write 'AGAINST." Then divide each page into three or four equal boxes. At the top of each box write your main idea for each paragraph, then use the rest of the space in each box to list facts or details that support that idea. Your two pages of notes might look like this:

Using Animals	for Scientific Tests
FOR	AGAINST
1. Gain in health benefits	1. Animals must be respected
2. Imprint discoveries made	2. Often unreliable results
3. Medical procedures tested	3. There are alternatives

When you have filled in the boxes, you will be able to tell if you have fairly presented both sides of the issue. If you notice that you have more information for one side, you will have to do some more research for the side with less material. The advantage of using this sort of graphic organizer is that it's practically an outline, so writing the outline that you will include with your report should be a breeze.

Writing the Draft

When you write a report on a social issue, the structure of your report will be different from the previous reports. Because you are reporting on two sides of an issue, you should be prepared to mention both sides in the introduction. I suggest that when you read over your notes, you look for a way to summarize each side of the issue in two or three sentences. You can then rephrase the introduction to include in your conclusion. Look back to page 45 for more information about writing an introduction and a conclusion to your report.

Another good idea is to see if you can phrase the title of your report in a question. For example, in the writing model that follows, you'll notice that the title is "Should We Use Animals for Scientific Tests?" By using a question as your title, you are likely to get your reader to think about where he stands on the issue. It's not important which side he is on. Your job as the writer is to present both sides fairly.

Revision Checklist

→ Have you been fair to both sides?

→ Have you given each side about the same amount of space?

→ Has your tone been fair throughout the report? Make sure that you don't have a mean-spirited tone in the part of your report that disagrees with the way you feel about the issue.

→ Can you follow the arguments for both sides of the issue? If not, perhaps you need to rethink or reorganize your report.

→ Do you begin each paragraph in the body of your paper with a general statement (topic sentence) that is supported with details in the paragraph?

SHOULD WE USE ANIMALS FOR SCIENTIFIC TESTS?

by Paul B. Janeczko

Social Studies

Ms. Perez

January 1, 2003

OUTLINE

I. Introduction.

    A. Animals have feelings and should not be subjected to cruelty.

    B. Advances in medical treatments would be impossible without animal testing.

II. Gains in human-health benefits outweigh animal suffering.

    A. Richard Pothier believes a human life is always more important than the life of a monkey.

    B. Surgeons practice on animals in med school.

III. Important medical discoveries came from animal testing.

    A. Louis Pasteur and others in mid-1800s.

    B. Scientists discovered vaccines for many diseases.

IV. Medical procedures are perfected on animals.

    A. Open-heart surgery came from twenty years of animal research.

    B. Many organ transplants are solved through animal testing.

V. Animal experiments may be important, but animals must be respected.

A. Jeffrey Masson believes animals do have feelings.

B. Their feelings might be more intense because they cannot speak.

VI. Experiments are often unreliable.

A. Some are not suited for modern medical problems.

B. They can, in fact, mislead researchers.

C. Stress changes animal physiology.

VII. Animal activists are outraged by some experiments.

A. Draize Test puts product in eyes of animals.

B. LD50 test sees how much product an animal needs before it dies.

VIII. There are alternatives to animal testing.

A. Lab tests that don't involve animals.

B. Synthetic skin.

C. Computer modeling.

IX. Conclusion.

A. Do animals have feelings?

B. Will humans suffer without animal testing?

C. The debate will go on.

SHOULD WE USE ANIMALS FOR SCIENTIFIC TESTS?

According to some estimates, 70 million animals are used in tests and experiments each year (Olesh). Animal rights activists believe that animals have feelings and should not be subjected to the cruelty and abuse of the lab. On the other hand, many scientists point to all the advances in modern medicine that would have been impossible without experimenting on animals. Both sides in the issue have a lot to say.

Many people who support animal testing believe that the gains in human health and well-being outweigh any animal suffering. Richard Pothier, who received a heart transplant, believes that a human life is always more important than the life of a monkey or a rabbit (*Newsweek*). Further, he is grateful that the surgeons who gave him a new heart had the opportunity to practice the procedure on animals in medical school.

Many important medical discoveries would not have been made possible without animal testing. Following the animal experiments in the mid-1800s by Louis Pasteur and others, scientists discovered the causes of many diseases and have developed vaccines to prevent these diseases, like rabies, whooping cough, tuberculosis, polio, measles, and mumps (Botting).

Medical procedures are often perfected by practicing on animals. Open-heart surgery, which saves about 440,000 lives each year in this country, is the result of twenty years of animal research. Organ transplants often present many complications, but animal research has been important in solving such problems (Botting).

Animal experiments are an important part of medical research. Scientists can control certain aspects of the animal's environment, like diet and living conditions, more than is usually possible with humans. Also, because the life cycle of many animals is shorter than human life, researchers can follow a subject through various stages of its life (Altweb).

While animal activists may acknowledge the important medical discoveries that have come from animal research, they feel that animals have their own lives and we have no right to use them as we wish. Jeffrey Masson, coauthor of *When Animals Weep: The Emotional Lives of Animals*, believes that animals feel pretty much all the emotions that humans do and maybe, in fact, more than humans because of their inability to speak (*E Magazine*).

Many medical doctors feel that animal experiments are too unreliable. Some experiments are poorly suited to dealing with the urgent health issues of our era (Barnard). Animal experiments can, in fact, mislead researchers or even contribute to illnesses and death by failing to predict the toxic effects of drugs. In addition, the stress of handling, confining, and isolating an animal changes its physiology and introduces other variables into the research (Barnard).

Animal rights activists are particularly outraged by the treatment of animals in testing of household products. For example, in the Draize Test, a test product — from soap to eye shadow — is dropped into an animal's eyes to see how the eye reacts over seventy-two hours.

Such tests often result in swollen eyelids, bleeding, and blindness ("All for Animals"). The LD50 (lethal dose) test is used to see how much of a product, like oven cleaner or furniture polish, will kill a percentage of a group of test animals over a period of time (PETA). The test product is force-fed to the animals, injected under their skin, or they are made to inhale it.

Those in favor of eliminating animal experiments point to alternatives to animal testing. The animal toxicity experiments used to test drugs like insulin have been mostly replaced by lab tests that do not involve animals. A synthetic skin is being studied as a possible replacement for animals to test a chemical's effect on skin. And computer modeling can replace some kinds of animal testing, like the dissection that takes place in high school biology classes (Altweb).

Do animals have feelings? Would it do humans a disservice if animal testing were ended? Both sides have legitimate arguments to support their opinions. More than likely, the debate between animal rights activists and those who favor animal testing will go on for some time.

BIBLIOGRAPHY

"All for Animals Newsletter." March, 1998. http://www .allforanimls.com/newsletter98.htm. January 5. 2002.

Barnard, Neal D., and Stephen R. Kaufman. "Animal Testing Is Wasteful and Misleading." Scientific

American Online. Feb. 1997.
http://www.sciam.com/0297issue/0297barnard.html.
January 5, 2002.

Botting, Jack H., and Adrian R. Morrison. "Animal
Research Is Vital to Medicine." Scientific American
Online. Feb. 1997.
http://www.sciam.com/0297issue/0297botting.html.
January 5, 2002.

FAQs. "Alternatives to Animal Testing on the Web."
http://www.altweb.jhsph.edu.education/FAQs.htm.

Olesh, Eric. "Animal Testing Should Be Allowed for
Household Products." (Essay 3 for Class)
http://www.inform.umd.edu/EdRes/Colleges/HONR/
HONR278B/hypernewsl.10/get/base/essay99-
3/23.html?nogifs. January 20, 2002.

Pothier, Richard. "Animal Tests Saved My Life."
Newsweek. Vol. 121, Feb. 1, 1993: 18.

"Product Testing: Toxic & Tragic." People for the Ethical
Treatment of Animals.
http://www.peta-online.org/mc/facts/fsae4.html.
January 25, 2002.

Singer, Karen. "The Inner Life of Animals." *E Magazine:
The Environmental Magazine*, Vol. 6, Sept.–Oct. 1995: 35.

CHAPTER SIX

Writing About a Place

in 1969 as the brainchild
vanted to open a recordi
illage in upstate New Yo
Bob Dylan. The businessm
attract a lot of attention
ometown. Although they h
s to risk money on t
vestors were interested
of this project that was
Music and Art F
Days of Peace a
t accommodate
end the fair, t
e was move
nsidered whi
passing any "m
lence" (American
peace singers like A
her acts were soon
rformers read like a
luding the Grateful
arwater Revival, and
o took pains to plan fo
ilities, and a medical st
t went into Woodstoc

When you're asked to write a report on a place, like a state, a country, or a region of a country, your first reaction might be panic. You might find yourself asking questions like, How can I write a short report about France (or Texas or the Panama Canal)?! There are entire books written about it. Well, the good news is that you're right: There is no way that you can write a short report and tell all there is to tell about a country. The better news is that if you are asking yourself these questions, it is a perfect way to start the process of writing a report on a place. When you recognize that you can't possibly write about a whole country, you can begin to think about how you will narrow your subject to a size that you can handle in a short report.

Getting Ideas

My first advice to you is: Think small. If you're supposed to write about a state, don't pick a big one like Texas or California. Pick a small one like Rhode Island or Vermont. If you're supposed to write about a country, don't pick the United States or China. Pick Belgium or Thailand. There will still be plenty of information written about a small country or state, but not nearly as much as there is written about a larger one.

Of course, as you are thinking about which small country or state to write about, look for one that appeals to you. Don't pick a subject just because it is small. Pick one in which you have some interest, even though that interest might be limited. For example, when I was trying to come up with a subject for the writing model for this chapter, I wanted to pick a country that intrigued me. Well, a lot of countries are interesting or mysterious — England, Scotland, Iceland, China, Poland, Australia, Bali, Italy — so I decided to pick a country that I might like to visit. Scotland came to mind. I have visited England twice but have never been to Scotland. Plus, I've been fascinated by the Loch Ness Monster for a long time, and I knew that Loch Ness (*loch* is the Scottish word for lake) is in the middle of Scotland. In fact, in the hope of visiting the country one day, I had received a packet of information from the British Tourist

Bureau. When I looked through the colorful booklet, filled with pictures of rolling hills and rocky coasts, I knew I would write this sample report about Scotland.

Another reason I liked my choice of Scotland was that the country is small — think small, remember? — so there wouldn't be too many books to consider for my research. And yet, even though Scotland is a small country — roughly the size of South Carolina — I knew there was still plenty that I could say about the country. Too much, in fact, for a short report, so I knew I had to narrow my subject.

The first thing I did to get some general information about Scotland was to check it out in *The World Book Encyclopedia*, which has an eleven-page article, complete with a map and some pictures. After I read through the article, I discovered that it ended with an outline of the article. The six main parts of the article were printed in bold type: government, people, way of life, the land, economy, and history.

With a good overview of Scotland, I checked the catalog at my library and found that there were only a few books on Scotland. Based on the information in the catalog, the book that seemed to best suit my needs was *Scotland*, a book in the Enchantment of the World series. Although the book is only about 125 pages, I didn't want to read all of it if I didn't need to. After all, like you, I only have so much time to research and write my report.

So, rather than read the whole book, I studied its table of contents, which is, by the way, something of an outline of a book. I compared the book's table of contents to the outline at the end of the encyclopedia article. As you would expect, there were some similarities between the two. And since what I had read and seen in the encyclopedia about the land itself reminded me of parts of Maine, the state in which I live, I decided to write my report about the geography of Scotland.

Research Tip

Geography Sources

One of the quickest and easiest ways to find information about a particular country is to do an online search. If you go to a search engine and type in the name of the country you are researching and put the word *tourism* after it — like "Scotland tourism" — you will find plenty of information. By adding *tourism* to your search, you will be eliminating other topics — such as politics, economics, industry — that you may not want to include in your report. You can follow the same procedure if you are researching a state.

In addition to researching information online, you should also visit the reference section of your library, where you will find atlases and geography books. If you type in the word *geography* and do a subject or key-word search of the library's catalog, you may find hundreds of books that might help you, especially if your library is part of a county system. Once you see all the books listed under geography, your first job is to look for the best books that will help you. A world atlas is also great to thumb through if you are unsure which country you would like to write about. Or, if you are going to report on a state, find a United States atlas and start browsing.

Another source of good information about a country or state is a guidebook, which offers much help to tourists visiting the place. In fact, chances are good that your library will include in its collection a wide array of guidebooks. And, if someone in your family is a member of an automobile club, like AAA, you can ask them to get you a guidebook from the club.

Taking Notes

Once I knew what my topic was, I could focus my research and note-taking. I reread the section on the land in *The World Book* article — it's barely half a page — and then I read the section on geography in *Scotland*. I figured those two sections would furnish the bulk of my notes for my report. I wound up taking notes from two other sources: the booklet on Scotland I received from the British Tourist Bureau and a Fodor's guidebook to the country. These four sources provided me with plenty of information.

One of the first things I noticed as I was taking notes is that the country is commonly said to be divided into three parts: the Border Country, the southern section that borders England; the Lowlands; and the Highlands and Islands. This gave me a sensible way to organize my notes as well as the report itself. So, as I took notes, I put my note cards into three piles, making sure that I had a source card for each source and that I marked the source-book code number of each note card. I wanted to make sure I knew where every note came from.

Getting Organized

Since I decided that I would divide my paper into three main sections — one for each of the geographic sections of Scotland — I drew a graphic organizer. I opened to a clean spread in my notebook and divided each page into two columns. At the top of the first three columns, I wrote the name of a section of the country: Border Country, Lowlands, Highlands and Islands. (The fourth column I divided into an upper and a lower half, just to give me space to jot down some notes for my introduction and conclusion.) With columns for each region of the country, I was able to organize my notes in the columns so I could see what information I had for each region. This graphic organizer made it easier for me to write an outline for the report.

Illustrations

I decided one more thing as I took notes. This is the type of report — more so than a report on a person or an event — that would benefit from some illustrations. I made sure that I included a map of Scotland on which I marked off with different colored highlighters the three sections of the country. And, as long as I was including a map, I decided to indicate on it the cities and landmarks that I mentioned in my report. In addition, I included a small, clear picture that illustrated the geography of each section of the country. Such visuals will allow the reader to better see the country about which I have written my report.

A Word About Craft

Combining Sentences

One of the quickest ways to bore your reader is to have too many short, choppy sentences. As you write your draft, look for those short sentences and see if you can combine some of them to make longer, more interesting sentences. Take a look at these short sentences from an early draft of my writing model on Scotland: "Scotland is a small country. It has many distinctive geographic characteristics. It also has many unique attractions." As I worked on the report, I combined those sentences into one sentence that I used to open my report: "Although Scotland is a relatively small country, it has many distinctive geographic characteristics and unique attractions." Can you see how the longer sentence flows more smoothly that those short sentences?

Here's another example: "Packed in this small country are three regions. They are called by different names. Each one has its own distinct characteristics." I combined those sentences this way: "Packed in this small country are three regions, called by different names, each with its own distinct characteristics."

Of course, it's okay to use short sentences in your report. Just be careful that you mix shorter and longer sentences.

Writing the Draft

Before you begin writing your draft, take a close look at your graphic organizer. Can you see a logical reason for why you put things where you did in your organizer? Can you clearly see what the major parts of your report will be? Do you have enough information to write your report? Make sure you can answer yes to these questions before you go on.

If you think your graphic organizer will lead you in the right direction in your report, take the information on the organizer and use it to write an outline. Remember that the outline will give you a more detailed plan for your report. Writing an outline is a good way to check if you have enough information. You can begin writing the draft of your report when you feel confident that you have what it takes to do a good job.

Revision Checklist

➡ Have you done a good job of explaining any geographic terms that the reader may be unfamiliar with?

➡ Have you included too many short, choppy sentences? If so, look for places where you can combine a few of them.

➡ Are there any confusing places that need to be clarified? A writing partner may be able to help you with this.

➡ Is your overall organization easy to follow?

➡ Have you checked for unrelated information that should be cut from your report? Include only details and facts that support a main point of your report.

SCOTLAND: LAND OF BENS, GLENS, AND LOCHS

by Paul B. Janeczko

Social Studies

Ms. Perez

January 1, 2003

OUTLINE

I. Introduction.

II. The Border Country.

   A. The countryside.

      1. River Tweed and Cheviot Hills.

      2. Rolling hills, moors, wooded valleys.

3. Site of Scott's Waverly novels.

4. Sunniest and driest places in Scotland.

B. Heart of industrial area.

    1. Glasgow, Scotland's largest city.

    2. Firth of Clyde, most important river.

    3. Ocean liner shipyards.

    4. Large bridges over Firth of Forth.

III. The Central Highlands.

A. Rugged and spectacular.

    1. Seventy-five percent mountains.

    2. Great Glen.

    3. Ben Novis, largest mountain in Great Britain.

    4. Loch Lomond, largest lake in Scotland.

    5. Loch Ness, home of Nessie.

B. Other attractions.

    1. Ideal for hikers, climbers, trail bikers.

    2. Balmoral Castle, summer home of royal family.

    3. Braemar, home of Highland Games.

    4. Kirriemuir, birthplace of J. M. Barrie.

IV. Northern Highlands.

A. Characteristics.

    1. Remote and wild.

    2. Ancient rock formations.

    3. Bronze and Iron Age villages.

    4. Favorite region for archaeologists.

B. The Islands.

    1. Outer Hebrides: no trees but lots of wildflowers.

2. Orkney Islands: greatest concentration of
   historic sites.
3. Shetland Islands: famous for its ponies.

V. Conclusion.

· ·

SCOTLAND: LAND OF BENS, GLENS, AND LOCHS

Although Scotland is a small country, it has many
distinctive geographic characteristics and unique
attractions. It occupies about the northern third of
Great Britain (*World Book*, 211). It is 274 miles long and
154 miles wide at its widest point, but only 25 miles
wide at its narrowest point. And despite the small size
of Scotland, it has about 2,000 miles of shoreline.
Packed in this small country are three regions, called
by different names, each with its own distinct
characteristics.

Because it borders England, the southern region of
Scotland is often called the Border Country. (It is also
called the Southern Uplands by some.) The sixty-mile
border is marked by the River Tweed and the Cheviot
Hills. This is a region of rolling hills, moors, and
wooded river valleys and farmlands (Fodor, 4). Roman
castles and English abbeys dot the hills of the Border
Country (*Scotland*, 17). In fact, near the abbey at
Melrose is Abbotsford, the home of Sir Walter Scott,
who included vivid descriptions of the area in his
Waverly novels. The area northwest of Edinburgh, the
capital of Scotland, contains some of the sunniest and

driest parts of Scotland, as well as sandy beaches and picturesque fishing villages (Fodor, 5).

This southern part of Scotland also contains the heart of the industrial area of the country (*Scotland*, 19). Glasgow, Scotland's largest city, is on the Firth of Clyde, Scotland's most important river (*World Book*, 217). (A firth is a large estuary.) In fact, it was on this firth that some of the world's finest ocean liners were built. The *Queen Mary*, the *Queen Elizabeth*, and the *Queen Elizabeth II* all steamed out to sea from the shipyards on the Clyde. Two large bridges span the Firth of Forth: a modern suspension bridge and an old-fashioned railroad bridge.

The Central Highlands are rugged and spectacular (Fodor, 5), with about seventy-five percent of the area made up of mountains. Great Glen (or valley) cuts through the highlands from Inverness to Fort Williams and is ringed by Scotland's tallest mountains, offering the most dramatic, captivating landscape in Scotland (Fodor, 5). Ben Novis (*ben* is the Scottish word for mountain), snow-capped, is the highest mountain in Great Britain, measuring 4,406 feet. This section of Scotland is also noted for its lochs (lakes), including Loch Lomand, the country's largest loch, and Loch Ness, which many people believe is inhabited by Nessie, the famous Loch Ness Monster.

Although there are popular vacation spots in this part of Scotland, it is not for sunbathers (*Scotland*, 18), since the temperature rarely goes above seventy degrees. However, it is ideal for hikers, mountain climbers, and bikers. Balmoral Castle, the summer residence of the British royal family, is located in Braemar, famous for the Highland Games. And southeast of the royal castle is the town of Kirriemuir, the birthplace of J. M. Barrie, author of *Peter Pan*.

The Northern Highlands are remote and wild (Fodor, 5) and offer towering cliffs, sea lochs, giant waterfalls, and steep glens. Near Sutherland and Caithness are stark, spectacular rock formations and remnants of ancient Bronze and Iron Age civilizations (*Scotland*, 24). The area is a favorite spot for archaeologists and bird-watchers.

The northern section of Scotland includes many islands. Off the western shore are the Outer Hebrides, a Norse word for islands on the edge of the ocean. There are no trees on these islands, but innumerable varieties of wildflowers. White beaches are backed by shell-sand pastures (called machairs) rich with wildflowers. Some say there are 1,000 varieties in Barra, the Garden of the Hebrides (*Scotland*, 24).

Six miles off the northern shore are the Orkney Islands, about seventy islands, although only about twenty of them are inhabited. However, found on these islands is the greatest concentration of prehistoric sites in Scotland (Fodor, 5), including the Stone Age village of Skara Brae (*Vacation Planner*, 42). Because these islands are so far north, winter days may be no more than five hours long, while beautiful summer days may last nearly twenty hours (*Scotland*, 24). The northernmost islands are the Shetlands, known, of course, for their ponies. This group of islands has the same latitude as the southern tip of Greenland and Siberia, but it is spared the Arctic weather because of the warming influence of the Gulf Stream (*Scotland*, 24).

Although Scotland is a small country, it is rich in different types of scenery and vegetation. From the rich and rolling farmland of the Border Country to the low and green Orkney Islands to the wild seascapes of the Western Isles, Scotland is a land of varied and natural beauty.

BIBLIOGRAPHY

Fodor's Scotland. New York: Fodor's Travel Publications, Inc., 1999.

"Scotland." *The World Book Encyclopedia*. Chicago: World Book, Inc., 1999.

Scotland Vacation Planner. Edinburgh: Scottish Tourist Bureau, 2001.

Sutherland, Dorothy B. *Scotland*. Chicago: Children's Press, 1994.

CHAPTER SEVEN

Writing a How-To Report

in 1969 as the brainchild
anted to open a recordi
illage in upstate New Yo
Bob Dylan. The businessm
attract a lot of attention
ometown. Although they h
s to risk money on t
vestors were interested
of this project that was
Music and Art F
Days of Peace a
t accommodate
nd the fair, t
e was move
nsidered wh
passing any "mu
lence" (American
peace singers like A
er acts were soon
rformers read like a
luding the Grateful
arwater Revival, and J
o took pains to plan f
ilities, and a medical st
t went into Woodstoc

H as this ever happened to you? You're trying to fix a flat on your bike, but you're having no luck, so you call a friend and ask for help. Your friend is perfectly willing to help you, but the instructions she gives just aren't very good. Maybe they're confusing. Or too brief because she assumes you know as much about bike repair as she does. Very discouraging, isn't it? Well, try to keep that scene in mind when you write a how-to report for your class. Remember, you need to be clear and patient and logical when you write your report.

Getting Ideas

Your first choice for a topic should be something that you're good at. Nobody wants to read a report on "How to Fix a Flat Tire on Your Bike" that is written by somebody who hasn't ridden a bike in five years and has never fixed a single flat tire. You can pick a topic that is practical, like fixing a flat tire, or you might choose a topic that is unique to you, like how to clean your room in record time.

It's a good idea to begin by listing some ideas in your writer's notebook. Take a clean page and write "HOW-TO REPORT" at the top. Then start writing down things you're good at. Try to be as specific as you can. For example, instead of writing that you are a good baby-sitter, you might write that you are great at preparing healthy snacks that the kids enjoy. Instead of saying that you have talent in arts and crafts, write that you make exciting collages or woven wall hangings. Can you think of other areas in which you do good things? Maybe in wood shop or in the kitchen. Do you have any collections? Does your mother brag about the way you wash the family car? Does your father rave about how you make his favorite peach tarts? Any of these would make a good subject for a how-to report.

On the other hand, your report could be about a subject about which you need to do research. For instance, you may have written a report for science on the importance of recycling and you'd like to write a how-to report about setting up a recycling program in your school. Or, if you've done a report on photographer-journalist Margaret Bourke White for art class, you might want to write your how-to report on making a pinhole camera. If you decide to write your report on a topic that requires you to do some research, don't forget that you need to acknowledge your sources within the text and in a bibliography at the end of the paper.

As you think about a topic, remember that you are writing a report and not making an instructional video. In other words, make sure that your process can be explained in words and your report doesn't wind up being a series of pictures for which you write captions. You might do a dynamite job wrapping birthday presents, but that process is much easier to show someone than it is to explain. On the other hand, some diagrams might help the reader visualize a difficult part of the process. For example, if you were writing a report on how to make a telegraph key, diagrams that show the wiring of the project would certainly be helpful to the reader.

Finally, choose a subject that you can intelligently write about for a few pages and not something that is too simple. For example, "How to Wash Clothes" might wind up like this:

First, you open the washing machine door. Next, you dump in the dirty clothes. Then you add the correct amount of detergent. Next, you close the washing machine door. Finally, you turn on the washing machine.

That's not much of a report, is it? You want yours to be better, and it will be when you find the right subject.

Getting Organized

Once you have selected the topic for your report, you might be well served if you use a graphic organizer to arrange the information in your report. Open your writer's notebook to a clean spread. At the top of the left page write "MATERIAL." At the top of the right page write "STEPS."

Next, you need to think the process through from beginning to end, and you should start writing down its steps. As you do this, picture the material that you need to complete the process. If you are baking a cake, your materials would include: a mixing spoon, a mixing bowl, water, oil, flour, a cake pan, measuring spoons, measuring cups. Make sure you list all the things you will need.

The best way to make sure that you don't miss a step along the way is to take notes while you actually perform the activity you are writing about. But if that's not practical, patiently and very carefully go through the process in your mind and jot down the steps. Remember that your reader will not know as much about the process as you do, so don't leave out a step, even though you might think, "Oh, it's not *that* important."

Research Interview

Research Tip

Although books, magazines, and the Internet are where you will find most of the information you will need to write a good report, keep in mind that you might have an excellent resource person right in your own neighborhood.

Suppose you're adept at fixing a lawn mower and you've decided that you want to write a how-to report on that. You think you can do it, but you might feel more confident about it if you could check it out with someone. Maybe you can visit a local small-engine repair shop and interview the manager to get the information you need. Or you want to write about making jewelry. You've made your share of necklaces and bracelets, but you want to find out how to make more complicated ones. Why not visit a local jeweler or jewelry-maker and ask some questions. Such research can be invaluable in adding authenticity to your how-to report.

If you decide that you want to do a research interview, make sure you call ahead and ask the person for permission to do an interview. Bear in mind that stores and shops may be busy at certain times during the day. For example, don't expect a chef to have time to talk to you during the lunchtime rush. When you call for an appointment, tell the person exactly what you would like from them. Don't ask a chef if you can watch her cook. Rather, ask if you could watch her make an omelet. Given advance notice, many people will be happy to assist you with a school assignment.

A Word About Craft

Using Transitional Words

One of the ways to make your writing smoother is to make sure you use transitional words between paragraphs and within the paragraphs as well. Such transitional words help you lead the reader from one step to the next. In a how-to report you'll be explaining a process, so you'll want to use transitional words like these: *first, second, third, next then, as soon as, when, afterward, immediately, before,* and *finally.*

If you look at the second paragraph of the Getting Organized section on page 125, you'll notice that I begin with the transitional word *next.* I begin the following sentence with the transitional phrase *as you do.* When you read the writing model, you will see that I use a few transitional phrases, like *before you begin, after you have gathered,* and *once you decide.* Phrases like these help the reader follow the steps in the process you are explaining.

Writing the Draft

Even though this report has more of a hands-on feel to it than reports on a social issue or about a person, it's still a report, so you need to pay attention to organization. Make sure that you have an introduction, a body, and a conclusion to your report. Each part is important.

In the introduction, you should get your reader's interest right away. You might do that by telling a brief anecdote. For example:

"Like many other code-making techniques, the use of invisible inks can be traced to ancient times. There are records that the Greeks and the Romans used invisible inks that they extracted from plants and nuts. However, you don't need to gather plants and nuts to make invisible inks. In fact, you probably have invisible inks around your house and don't even know it."

You can also open with a question that hooks your reader. Here's an example:

"What would you say if I told you that you probably have some invisible inks around your house and don't even know about it? Would you believe me if I told you that you have probably drunk some invisible ink at some time in your life? These questions might sound crazy to you, but that's because you don't know that some common foods, drinks, and household products make excellent invisible inks."

The body of your report will include all the information that your reader will need to complete the process you are explaining. As you write, remember to help the reader follow your sequence of steps. One way to do that is to number the steps in the order in which they will be done. Make sure you include appropriate transitional words.

It's a good idea to alert your readers to any potential problems that they might encounter during the process. For example, if you are writing a how-to book about baking, you can warn your readers that if the water for the yeast is too warm, the yeast will not work. Of course, you should also offer advice to your readers, like suggesting that they place the pie on a cookie sheet when it is baking to prevent any of the juices from spilling onto the bottom of the oven.

The conclusion could be a summing up of the important part of the process, or it might be more of an anecdotal ending, perhaps something like this:

"Although making an invisible ink is not very hard, finding the right solution takes a little practice and patience. But once you have found the right ink, you will have no trouble sending secret messages."

Revision Checklist

➡ Is the sequence of steps in your report clear?

➡ Can the reader easily move from one step to the next?

➡ Have you included any information that will distract the reader from successfully completing the process? If you notice any, cut it out of your report.

➡ Can you find any places where adding a transitional word or phrase would make the steps easier to follow?

➡ Have you alerted the reader to any potential problems she might encounter along the way?

HOW TO MAKE AND USE INVISIBLE INKS
by Paul B. Janeczko
Language Arts Class
Ms. Perez
January 1, 2003

OUTLINE

  I. Introduction.

 II. Equipment.

      A. Various "pens."

      B. Small storage containers.

      C. Paper.

III. Invisible inks.

      A. Fruit juices that need not be diluted.

      B. Powders that need to be diluted.

IV. Writing with invisible ink.

A. Write out your message.

B. Diluting ink may be necessary.

V. Developing invisible ink with heat.

VI. How to send invisible ink message.

A. Do not send a "blank" sheet of paper.

B. Write between lines of real message.

C. Write along edge of newspaper.

VII. Conclusion.

HOW TO MAKE AND USE INVISIBLE INKS

Like many other code-making techniques, the use of invisible inks can be traced to ancient times. There are records that the Greeks and the Romans used invisible inks that they extracted from plants and nuts. However, you don't need to gather plants and nuts to make invisible inks. In fact, you probably have invisible inks around your house and don't even know it.

Before you begin to make invisible inks, you need to make sure you have all the equipment you will need. First of all, you will need instruments to write with. You could use a quill — a feather with the end carved to look like a pen point — toothpicks, or a small brush, like the ones you use with watercolors. Although it will take some practice, a brush makes a good "pen" because it will not leave indentations in the paper, a sure giveaway of your invisible-ink secret. Next, you will need a few small containers with lids, like baby-food jars or the small plastic canisters that 35-mm film comes in. As far as paper is concerned, the less glossy the paper, the better to use with invisible ink.

After you have collected your equipment, you can start gathering your ink. As I said, you will be able to find some invisible inks in your own house. The following make fine invisible inks: apple juice; citrus juice, like lemon and orange; onion juice (it might take a few tears to mash enough onions to get some ink, but it does work); and vinegar. All of these liquids you can use "straight," that is, without diluting them.

Other invisible inks can be made by dissolving any of the following in a glass of water:

- a teaspoon of honey or sugar
- salt or Epsom salt
- baking soda

Once you decide which invisible ink you'd like to use, pour a little bit of it into a small paper cup. Dip your "pen" — a toothpick, for example — into the ink and write out your message. If you can see your writing on the page you must dilute your invisible ink a bit so you cannot see it on the page. For example, if you can see the apple juice, mix in a little water until you cannot see the writing. All of these invisible inks should disappear when they have dried.

To develop your message, you need to apply direct heat to the paper. You can use a hair dryer, a small heater, an iron on a low setting, or a lightbulb of about

about 150 watts. Be careful you don't get burned by any of these heat sources. All you need to do is hold your message about six inches away from the heat and give it a little bit of time to work. Before long, your message will appear, as if by magic.

Once you have created a suitable invisible ink, you want to use it in a way that will keep your message secret. You should not write a message on a blank sheet of paper and give it to your friend. If it should fall into the wrong hands, the blank page will be a giveaway that it contains a message written in invisible ink. The best way to use your invisible ink is to write your message on a page that already has writing or printing. For example, you can write your friend a letter in regular ink, then write your invisible ink message in the spaces between the lines of the letter. Or, you can write your message in the blank space along the edge of a newspaper page.

Although making an invisible ink is not very hard, finding the right solution takes a little practice and patience. But once you have found the right ink, you will have no trouble sending secret messages written in invisible ink. And you can do it with "inks" that you can find in your own home!

in 1969 as the brainchild
...vanted to open a recordi...
...llage in upstate New Yo...
...Bob Dylan. The businessm...
...t attract a lot of attention...
...ometown. Although they h...
...s to risk money on t...
...estors were interested...
...of this project that was...
...Music and Art F...
...Days of Peace a...
...t accommodate...
...nd the fair, t...
...e was move...
...nsidered wh...
...passing any "m...
...lence" (American...
...opeace singers like A...
...her acts were soon...
...rformers read like a...
...cluding the Grateful D...
...earwater Revival, and J...
...o took pains to plan f...
...cilities, and a medical st...
...t went into Woodstoc...

CHAPTER EIGHT

Writing a Science Report

We live in an amazing world. Look around. Whether you live in a city or in the country, amazing things are going on. The natural world is full of wonder. And a science report is the perfect place for you to explore some of that wonder. A science report can examine a topic, like ecosystems, black holes, and magnets. It can explore the life of a famous person of science, like Madame Curie or Alexander Graham Bell. Or it can give your account of a scientific experiment. The choice is yours.

Getting Ideas

For starters, I would suggest that you set aside a page or two in your writer's notebook and write "I WONDER" at the top of the page. Use this space to write down any ideas that might come to you as you go about your day (and night). Many of the things you write down may be questions about things you wonder about, as in, Why does the moon change shape each month? or, Where do birds go in the winter and how do they get there? or, How does electricity work? or, How do they get the music on a CD? If you can come up with a good question, you can do research and write a report to answer that question.

Another way to get ideas for your science report is to keep your eyes and ears open when you read a magazine or a newspaper or when you watch TV or a movie. You might very well come across something that you can use as the basis for your report. For example, you might see a magazine article about the planes that fly right into the middle of hurricanes and wonder why anyone would do that. (You can paste any interesting articles in your notebook, too.) Or you might watch a movie with computerized animation and wonder how computers can draw. Or on the evening news you might catch a story on fiber optics and learn that Alexander Graham Bell experimented with the transmission of sound on a beam of light, the precursor of fiber optics, and decide that you want to find out more about him. Find a subject that interests you — even if only a little — and see what you can learn about it. If you are interested in the subject, it will be easier for you to get someone else excited about that subject.

I got the idea for my writing model here a few years ago when I was reading a book called *The Discoverers*, written by Daniel J. Bocrstin. It's a great book about the people who made discoveries that changed the way we look at the world, from the solar system to the nervous system. One item that I found fascinating was the fact that the early mechanical clocks in the Middle Ages didn't have faces or hands. They simply chimed the hour. This was important to the monks, because at certain hours during the day, they needed to pause in their work and go to the chapel for prayers. That little fact made me wonder what ancient people did to tell time. And that led me to investigate early clocks.

Focusing Your Search

Research Tip

When you think you know what you'd like to write your science report about and start to do your research, don't be too narrow in your search. For example, when I started my research, I looked up "clock" because I knew that was what my report was going to be about. It didn't take me long to realize that many books on clocks are listed under the subject heading of "time," which gave me something else to look up. I also found some helpful information in a book about inventions. So, when you start researching, be open to possibilities beyond the specific word that names your subject.

Getting Organized

If you look back to the first page of this chapter, you will notice that I believe that there are times when good ideas for reports come in the form of a question. If you look closely at my questions, you'll see that a number of them ask you to show how A resulted in B. For example, How do they get music on a CD? To answer this question is to show the problem that sound technicians faced as they worked to perfect digital sound recording. Many of the better science topics could be explained in a cause-effect report. My sample report on early clocks is, in fact, a cause-effect report. Certain problems—telling the time when there is no sun, for example—caused the development of water clocks.

To help you organize your material for such a cause-effect science report, you might want to make a chart that shows the various causes and effects of your topic. For example, here are a few of the causes and effects that I include in my report:

CAUSES			EFFECTS
Monks needed to know hour for prayer	○	○	Developed clock
Egyptians needed to track celestial bodies			Invented astrolabe
Greeks needed to tell time at night	○	○	Invented water clock

In fact, sometimes it is interesting (and helpful) to see the effect and to look for the cause that led to that effect. Many inventions were the result of specific problems that the inventor tried to solve. The telephone, for example, was the effect of Alexander Graham Bell trying to find a way to transmit voice over distances. The polio vaccine was the result of Dr. Jonas Salk's determination to end the horrors of polio.

Writing the Draft

Often a science report will tell a story. It might be the story of how clocks were invented. It might be the story of how Marie Curie and her husband, Pierre, worked with radioactivity. It might be how ancient mathematicians puzzled over solid figures, like the cube. So, as you are writing your report, keep in mind that you are telling a story and try to make that story as interesting as you can. That means including interesting, even startling, facts in your report.

Although the facts and information that you include in a science report are important, don't forget about the story that you're telling. Try to make it compelling. One way to make your story compelling is to make sure that one part of your story leads smoothly to the next part of your story. You don't want your reader scratching his head and looking back at some earlier paragraphs in your report for some missing piece. So, as you write your report, ask yourself if you can see how each cause leads to an effect. Don't be surprised if an effect then becomes the cause of another effect. For example, in my report, the Greeks created sundials to tell time; however, sundials didn't work when the sun wasn't shining. So, the sundial, once an effect, became the cause for finding a way to tell time at night, which led to the water clock.

A Word About Craft

Cause-Effect Transitional Words

Because your cause-effect science report may also be something of a narrative, you'll need to be careful to include appropriate transitional words or phrases to get from one part of the report to the next. Some of these cause-effect transitional expressions would include *because*, *since*, *therefore*, *so that*, and *as a result*. Some of the transitional words that show time are *finally*, *before*, *after*, *next*, and *then*. Such words and phrases, though seemingly unimportant, serve the invaluable function of helping your reader move smoothly along in your report from one thought to another.

Revision Checklist

→ Is the connection between a cause and an effect clear?

→ Do I need to rearrange some parts of a sentence or passage to make the connection clearer?

→ Do my transitional words help the reader move from one part of the paper to the next?

→ Is the time sequence clear?

→ Have I developed all my ideas?

→ Do I need to add some information to make my ideas clear?

→ Do my sentences sound pretty much alike, or have I written a variety of sentence types?

EARLY CLOCKS AND HOW THEY WORKED
by Paul B. Janeczko
Science
Ms. Perez
January 1, 2003

OUTLINE

   I. Introduction.

  II. Earliest clocks.

      A. Egyptian star-clock charts.

      B. Greek astrolabe.

 III. Early sun clocks.

      A. Obelisk (sun stick).

      B. Shadow clock.

 IV. Sundials.

      A. Early models made of stone.

      B. Hemicycle of about 300 B.C.

  V. Water Clocks.

      A. Created for King Amenophis I of Egypt.

      B. Early design.

      C. Greeks make improvements.

         1. A float told time.

         2. Water-controlled gizmos on clock.

         3. Adjustments for water pressure.

 VI. Conclusion.

EARLY CLOCKS AND HOW THEY WORKED

It might be hard to imagine, but clocks have been around for nearly 4,000 years (James, 124). However, before the fourteenth century clocks didn't have hands. We are used to clocks without hands — in fact, you may have a digital watch on your wrist right now — but the Egyptians, the Greeks, and the Romans created several early clocks that weren't nearly as portable as your digital watch.

The earliest clocks relied on the stars to tell time. The Egyptians made star-clock charts from which time could be calculated by seeing which stars had already risen (James, 124). The Greeks later invented the astrolabe to measure the altitudes of celestial bodies. The measurement of the altitude of the sun and stars allowed the Greeks to determine the time (*Grolier*).

Egyptians used the sun to determine the time. They placed a stick in the ground and marked off the hours around the stick. Cleopatra constructed a large elaborate obelisk — a shape like the Washington Monument — in the community center that functioned as a giant sun stick (*Science*, 581). They also created a shadow clock in which the shadow of a crossbar gradually crossed a series of marks as the sun set (James, 124). The Egyptian shadow clock was small and could easily be carried around (Burns, 30). You can see that both of these devices were ancestors of the sundial.

The Greeks and the Romans made much use of the sundial. Although sundials were still made of stone, they became more sophisticated in design and varied in form. One of the best and most common sundial was the hemicycle of Berosus, which dates from about 300 B.C. It was a hollowed-out bowl, which was placed so it faced south. Lines on its inner surface corresponded to the twelve hours of the day. A horizontal gnomon cast a shadow on the correct hour (*Americana*, 89).

Water clocks can be traced to the Egyptians. Some people believe that the Egyptian priests needed to know the time at night so rituals and sacrifices of the temple could be carried out at the proper time (James, 124). Others believe the story that is told of how King Amenophis I wanted to be able to tell the time without the inconvenience of getting out of bed and consulting his star charts. Prince Amenemhet solved the problem by creating a water clock (Burns, 34).

The Greek word for such a clock is *clepsydra*, which means thief of water. At first it was simply a stone jar or jug of water with a small hole in the bottom, so that water dripped out drop by drop (Brearley, 50). An Egyptian water clock that dates from 1380 B.C. was an alabaster bowl with sloping sides and a small hole at the bottom from which a small metal outlet pipe protruded (*Americana*, 89). Etched on the inside of the vessel were rings that indicated the passing of each hour. Someone who wanted to know the time could consult the rings or could even put her hand in the jar and estimate the time.

Not all water clocks were that simple. Athens had a town clock at about 350 B.C. in which the movements of the clock were controlled by a float, which sank as the water level lowered. The float was probably connected to a shaft, which moved a pointing hand as it fell (James, 125). Another elaborate Greek water clock dates from 270 B.C. Its water outflow drove all sorts of gizmos, from ringing bells and moving puppets to singing birds — perhaps an early cuckoo clock! (James, 125).

The Greeks discovered a problem with the traditional water clock, but they managed to solve it. They noticed that, because of water pressure, water ran faster from a full jar than from one that was nearly empty. They solved this problem with a double vessel. The larger one below contained a float that rose as the jar filled, marking the hours. To make sure the water clock was accurate, the top jar needed to be constantly filled to the brim (Brearley, 52).

Modern clocks have come a long way since the time of the sundial and the water clock. Now we have quartz clocks and atomic clocks. But regardless of how much more accurate our clocks have become, we must recognize the contributions ancient people made to the science of telling time.

BIBLIOGRAPHY

"Astrolabe." *Grolier Multimedia Encyclopedia.* Danbury, CT: Grolier Interactive Inc., 1998.

Brearley. Harry C. *Time Telling Through the Ages* New York: Doubleday, Page & Co., 1919.

Burns, Marilyn. *This Book Is About Time*. Boston: Little, Brown, 1978.

"Clock." *Encyclopedia Americana*. Danbury, CT: Grolier Inc., 1996.

"Clock." *The Illustrated Science and Invention Encyclopedia*. Westport, CT: H.S. Stuttman Inc., 1983.

"Clocks and Watches." *Grolier Multimedia Encyclopedia*. Danbury, CT: Grolier Interactive Inc., 1998.

James, Peter, and Nick Thorpe. *Ancient Inventions*. New York: Ballantine, 1994.

Other Possibilities

Although my writing model here is about looking at the development of clocks from a scientific point of view, there are other types of science reports that you can write. Of course, the type of report you write will depend on the requirements of your teacher. She may want you to write a report on some sort of scientific experiment that you've conducted in class or on your own. If she does, you might find some help in the section in this guide called "Writing a How-To Report" (see page 123). The steps and suggestions that I give for that report should help you if you need to write a report about an experiment, which basically describes the steps you took and the results you experienced.

Your teacher may allow you to write about one of the important persons of science. If that's the case, you can consider the advice I gave in the section "Writing a Report About a Person in History" (see page 79). In that chapter, my sample paper is about Rosa Parks. I emphasize her work in the civil rights movement because that's where she made her greatest contributions. Although the process about writing about a person of science would be the same, the emphasis would be on the contributions that person made to the world of science.

CHAPTER NINE

Writing a Book Report

in 1969 as the brainchild
vanted to open a recordi
illage in upstate New Yo
Bob Dylan. The businessm
attract a lot of attention
ometown. Although they h
s to risk money on t
estors were interested
of this project that was
Music and Art Fe
Days of Peace a
t accommodate
end the fair, t
e was move
nsidered wh
passing any "m
lence" (American
peace singers like A
er acts were soon
rformers read like a
luding the Grateful
arwater Revival, and
o took pains to plan f
ilities, and a medical st
t went into Woodstoc

I 've written my share of book reviews for magazines, and I've come to realize that they are really book reports. Oh, they're longer than the book reports I wrote when I was your age, but they're still very similar. The book reports that you'll have to write for class will probably be one of three kinds: a summary of a book, a critical book report, or an analysis of a character in a novel or play.

I know that you're writing a book report to get a grade from your teacher. I also know that you're more than likely trying to convince your teacher that you actually read the book you are reporting on. If this is the case, let me suggest a slight attitude adjustment. I think you'll find writing a book report more satisfying if you focus on a different audience. Instead of thinking that you're writing for your teacher, try to imagine that you are writing the book report to convince a good friend to read this book. Such a shift in audience might help you bring more enthusiasm to the project.

Have you ever thought of each book report as part of a record of the books you have read? I know a number of people who keep careful, dated records of the books they've read. Some make notes on file cards and keep them in a little box. Others write longer "book reports" and organize them in a three-ring binder. Some high-tech friends save all their book-reading notes and opinions on a disk or in a folder in their computers. I suspect that you've read quite a few books in your life already, so this might be a good time to give some thought to keeping track of your reading. Over time, as you read back over your book files, you may notice how your tastes in reading have changed. You might also recall some of your favorite books and decide to read them again.

Be an Active Reader

Before you start reading your book, make sure you understand what your teacher expects in the book report. Different teachers have different expectations, and not knowing what your teacher expects from you is no excuse for writing an inferior book report. Can you report on any book you wish? Fiction or nonfiction? Must you choose a book from a list furnished by your teacher? What kind of book report are you being asked to write? Does your teacher expect a minimum length for the report? Does she have a particular format that she wants the class to follow? Handwritten or typed? Does she allow you to include your opinion of the book? And then comes the big question, When is it due?

When you do start to read your book, remember that you have a better chance of writing a good book report if you are an active reader. What is an "active reader"? A person who reads carefully. An active reader thinks, feels, reacts, and makes conclusions while she reads. An active reader makes notes on a book along the way, maybe underlining parts of the book she wants to remember (only, of course, if you are reading a book that you own). These notes will be invaluable when you are ready to write a book report.

When I review a book, I use a 6" x 8" index card as a bookmark. Before I start to read a book, I write the title of the book and the author's name on the top line of the index card. I learned that little trick one day in my office when I knocked over a stack of books and a pile of file cards filled with notes on the books, and realized that I had not written the title of the book or even the name of the author on any of the cards. As I looked at the debris scattered on the floor, I wondered why I'd not taken the ten seconds to write the title of each book on the cards. Of course, it took me quite a while to match the cards to the right books. From that time on, I made sure that simple, vital information is the first thing I write on the file card before I take a single note.

Your writer's notebook is also an excellent place to write down your reading notes. The advantage of keeping your notes in your writer's notebook is that you can keep them all in one place, although it does mean that you need to keep your notebook handy when you are reading your book.

Make a Schedule

Once you know when the book report is due, you can make a schedule that gives you enough time to read the book and write a top-notch report. To set a realistic schedule, you need to be honest with yourself. Only you know how fast you can read. Make sure that you actually write out your timetable on your calendar. Just don't glance at the calendar and tell yourself that you'll have plenty of time to read the book and write your report. If your teacher has assigned a due date for an outline and a first draft, write those on the calendar. Check to see how many pages are in the book. Then, considering all your other obligations, figure out how many pages of the book you can reasonably read each day. Mark those page numbers on the calendar. Take a close look at the calendar and make sure that it looks doable to you. If it doesn't, tinker with it until you come up with something you can live with.

When you are satisfied with the schedule, try your best to stick with it. If you get ahead of your scheduled reading, good for you! You can reward yourself with a night off to hang out with your friends or watch a video you've been dying to see. Or you can keep reading and get ahead of your schedule. In my opinion, it never hurts to be ahead of schedule. It is a good insurance policy to have in case some unexpected event pops into your life. Plus, think how impressed your teacher will be if you actually hand in your well-written book report a few days early!

Start to Read

Whenever I read, I always keep a pen and pad handy. I'm an underlining nut. (Only in my books!) I underline words and phrases that I want to remember, for whatever reason. Maybe a poetic line. Maybe a thought that I want to remember. Maybe a vocabulary word that I want to look up to make sure I understand its meaning. Does it slow down my reading? Sure, but only a little bit. That little bit of extra time is time well spent because it helps me understand and remember the book.

What things should you be on the lookout for as you read? That will depend to some degree on what kind of book report you need to write. Later I will make specific suggestions for different types of book reports. However, as a general rule, I would advise you to concentrate on what is important and memorable to you in the book.

As you take notes while you read, remember that they are merely your notes, not something that you are going to hand in. So don't worry about getting your notes perfectly neat. The best notes are the ones that help you write a great book report. Here are some suggestions:

Look for the main events of the story. Especially those turning points that every good story has. Who are the characters in the book? How would you describe them with a few adjectives? How are they related to other characters? As you write down the important events of a novel, you might also make notes about which ones are your favorites. You should also notice how the story makes you feel. Do you feel sorry for a character when something unfortunate happens to her? Does a part of the book scare you? Are you relieved when the main character is reunited with his father? Are you disappointed with the ending? These are all points that you might include in your book report. Do the events of the story remind you of something that happened to you or a friend? Or to someone in your family?

If you are reading a nonfiction book, you will be most concerned with what the author wants you to think about his subject. Is he simply giving you information or does he have a point to make? For example, the author of one nonfiction book about mammals might simply give you lots of facts about mammals, while another author might want you to see from the facts that more and more species are becoming extinct. Beyond that, when you are reading a nonfiction book, you will be looking for facts of all kinds. Fun facts, frightening facts, amazing facts. You can also be looking for information that reminds you of something else in your life. For example, a book on recycling that gives you all sorts of facts about trash and waste might remind you about all the junk mail your household receives, or motivate you to encourage your Girl Scout troop to have a recycling drive.

To write a convincing book report, no matter which kind, you'll need to be an active reader. There's no substitute for reading carefully and taking good notes. Be willing to ask yourself questions about what happens in the book and why you think it happens. Be ready to jot down your answers in your writer's notebook.

When You've Finished Reading

When you have finished reading your book, you should do three things.

→ First of all, you should pat yourself on the back for what you've done: You've finished the book and learned more about a specific subject or about human nature. Ideally, you will be right on schedule, too. And, you've completed the first part of writing a book report: reading the book!

→ Next, you should take a little time to write down your impressions of the book, while they're still fresh in your mind. Start a new page of your notebook and write down the first things that come to your mind about what happened in the book and how you felt about the book.

→ Finally, if you're ahead of schedule, give yourself a day off. You've earned it. This little breather will help you get ready for the work that is yet to come.

CHAPTER TEN

Writing a Summary of a Book

n some ways, writing a summary of a book is the easiest kind of book report to write. If you are an active reader, that is. If you read a novel quickly and mindlessly, anxious for the book to be finished, you'll have a difficult time remembering what happened in the novel, let alone trying to write about it. However, if you are an active, note-taking reader, not only will the report be easier to write, it will be a better report.

Getting Ideas

The best way to take notes for a summary book report is to read with your notebook by your side. I suggest you open it to a place where you have two blank facing pages. At the top of the left-hand page, write "CHARACTERS." You'll use that page to write notes about the major characters in the novel. When you come across a character for the first time, write his or her name, then write what you learn about this character the first time he appears in the novel. You could include physical characteristics, like hair color or the way he or she walks. Leave a few lines blank so you can include more information as you continue reading. Then write the name of the second character you meet in the novel, and do the same for that one. Remember to give yourself some extra space so you can add information as you continue to read.

At the top of the right-hand page, write "PLOT." In the left-hand margin, write "Chapter 1." You can take notes on the plot of the novel in any way that works best for you. You can write phrases that give details for different things that happens. You can write each action out in a complete sentence. As is the case for all note-taking, you want to keep what you write to a minimum, but you want to make sure that you give yourself enough useful information to use in your book report. This means that you can abbreviate names of characters. Since the main characters in William H. Armstrong's novel *Sounder* are not named, I used B for the boy, F for his father, M for his mother, and S for the dog, Sounder. But, before you move on to a new chapter, it's a good idea to write a brief summary of each chapter as you finish it.

When should you take notes? That's up to you. It depends on what kind of a reader you are. When I was taking notes for my writing model, I wrote down my notes when I finished reading a chapter. The chapters are short enough that I was able to do that. Some readers take notes as they are reading a chapter. Others don't like to interrupt the flow of the story by stopping to take notes. Decide which method works best for you. If you're not sure, try it both ways and go with the choice that you're comfortable with. Keep in mind that you might change your note-taking method the next time you need to write a book summary if, for example, the chapters are longer or more complicated. But don't wait until you have read several chapters before you start taking notes. You might forget some crucial information if you don't make note of it right away.

If you keep your notebook open in front of you while you read, you will be able to take notes on the characters in the book as well as on the plot—the action of the story. Since your notes are supposed to help you remember the elements of a novel, feel free to use them in a way that does help you. Don't be afraid to draw lines, let's say, between characters that are related, or from the name of a character to a chapter in which he first appears or takes some important step. You should also jot down page numbers that you might want to refer to later on, maybe those of a crucial scene in the novel or something important that a character said. Make notes in whatever way will help you remember what happens in the novel.

Getting Organized

By the time you have finished reading your novel, you should have several pages filled with information about characters as well as a three- or four-sentence summary of each chapter. Consider them the same as the notes you took when you were researching a subject for a report for another class. Once you have good notes, you need to find the best way to organize those notes. True, your notes reflect the order in which the events happen in the novel, but you still need a way to make sure they tell the story of the novel seamlessly.

One way to organize your material is to jot down the major events in the story along a time line, which is called a plot diagram. It is something like the time line that I suggested earlier in this guide (see page 87). However, while the other time lines will be a straight horizontal line, a plot diagram reflects the rising action and falling action of a novel and looks like this:

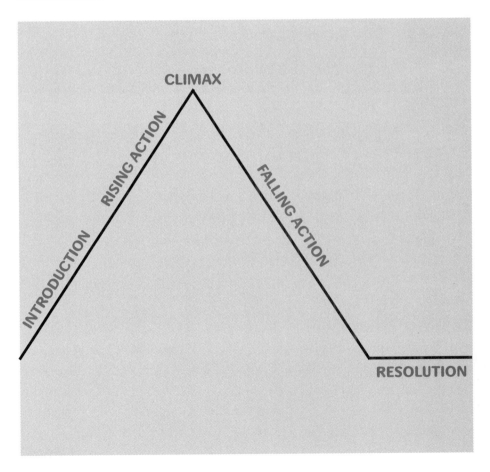

CLIMAX

RISING ACTION

FALLING ACTION

INTRODUCTION

RESOLUTION

As you can see, I've included on the diagram the five parts of a novel: introduction, rising action, climax, falling action, resolution. Keep in mind that your actual diagram may very well look different from the one above. The climax is always near the end of a novel, but in some novels it will come at the very end of the book, while in other novels it may come a chapter or two before the end.

Plotting the main events of your novel along a plot diagram will help you recognize how some of the events early in the story are related to the climax, something that you will want to mention when you write your summary. And a plot diagram will also help you recognize those events that are truly pivotal in the story and, therefore, need to be part of your summary.

When you draw your plot diagram, don't be afraid to spread it across two pages of your notebook. This will give you plenty of room to include all the main events of the story. You don't want to leave any of them out of your report just because you crowded your plot diagram onto a single page in your notebook.

A Word About Craft

Summarizing

Writing a good summary is about choosing the most important elements of a novel and incorporating them in a coherent book report. You want to make sure that your summary includes the who, what, where, when, and why of the novel.

➡ Who: Include the most important characters in a novel as well as any relationships they might have with other characters. *Sounder* is a pretty simple story with only a handful of characters and no relationships that are not obvious.

➡ What: In the introduction of your report you should mention what the theme or main idea of the novel is. In the introduction to my report,

I mention that the author, Armstrong, explores the issue of survival. Specifically, can a poor black boy survive in a world of cruelty and hatred. Frequently, a book will have multiple themes, but you need mention only the most important ones in a summary.

→ Where: Armstrong never specifically tells the reader where the story takes place. We do know that it does take place somewhere in the Deep South, and that is enough for us to realize that it was a place filled with racial bigotry. Place might be more important in historical novels, for example, or in novels where specific landmarks figure in the action of the story.

→ When: As with the place of the novel, Armstrong is not specific because the exact time in which the story takes place is not important to the action. Because the characters travel on foot or in horse-drawn wagons, we know that it doesn't take place in modern times. That's really all we need to know. But in other novels the time of the action is important. For example, it's important to know that *The Red Badge of Courage* takes place during the Civil War.

→ Why: What is the motivation for the main characters to act as they do? In some cases, you might not know exactly why, but if you think as you read, the motivation of the characters will become clearer to you.

Writing the Draft

If you've taken good notes as you read your novel and placed the main events of the story properly along your plot diagram, you should have no trouble writing the draft of your summary. Remember that a summary of a book doesn't include your opinion of the characters or of the story. You are simply trying to let your reader know what happens to whom in the novel. When you write a critical book report or write about a character in a book, you'll be able to include your opinions since the purpose of those types of reports is to let the reader know your feelings and opinions about the novel and its characters.

As you write your draft, concentrate on getting the events of the story in the correct order. Follow your notes and your plot diagram. If you get confused about exactly what happened to whom in the novel, go back to the book and check it out. If you have included page numbers in your notes, they'll help you locate the part of the novel that you are uncertain about. Keep the events in the right order and, unless your teacher has told you otherwise, it's okay to reveal the ending of the novel. Chances are your teacher has read the novel you are reporting on and already knows the ending.

Revision Checklist

→ Have you chosen the most important events in the novel and retold them in the order in which they appeared in the novel?

→ Have you identified the major characters? Have you included these characters in your summary?

→ Have you paid attention to transitional words and phrases that show time? Some of these most common words and phrases are *soon, later, afterward, immediately, finally, then, next, as soon as, when, before, during,* and *after.* Check that you have used such transitional words and phrases appropriately.

→ Does your introduction include a statement on the theme of the novel? In other words, have you thought about the main idea in the novel?

A Summary Book Report:

Sounder, by William H. Armstrong

by Paul B. Janeczko

Language Arts

Ms. Perez

January 1, 2003

Although the title of this book is the name of the hound dog in the story, the book is really more about the young boy than it is about the dog. *Sounder* is the story of how the young boy grows up in the absence of his father, who is imprisoned for stealing a ham to feed his poor family. Along the way, the boy must deal with poverty, racism, and loneliness. It is the love of his mother and the kindness of the schoolmaster that help the boy deal with hatred and loss.

The novel opens with a black man and his son standing on the porch of a sharecropper's cabin in the Deep South. The cabin is far from other cabins, the meetinghouse, and the school, which were "far away at the edge of town." The boy starts talking about Sounder, the dog that was "a mixture of Georgia redbone hound and bulldog." When he trees a coon or possum, "his voice would roll across the flatlands. It wavered through the foothills, louder than any other dog's in the whole countryside."

The poor family relies on the hound to help bring in money when he goes hunting with the father. The family receives "fifty cents for a possum and two dollars for a coonhide," which the mother uses for "flour and overall jackets with a blanket lining." The mother shells walnuts to sell at the store in town. She gathers them when they fall after the first hard frost. She shells two pounds per night and is paid fifteen cents per pound "if they're mostly half-kernels and dry."

Things suddenly change for the family when the sheriff and two deputies arrive to arrest the father for stealing a ham from a smokehouse. They snap handcuffs on the father's wrists and roughly drag him out to the wagon. Sounder starts growling and scratching at the door. The deputy warns the boy, "Go out and hold that mongrel if you don't want him shot." When they load the father into the wagon and ride away, Sounder breaks loose and runs for the wagon. One of the deputies turns in his seat and fires his shotgun at the dog. Sounder falls in the road. The boy "wanted to cry; he wanted to run to Sounder. His stomach felt sick; he didn't want to see Sounder." The dog runs to hide under the porch, but the boy could see that the shotgun blast "had torn off the whole side of his head and shoulder." The boy calls to Sounder, but the dog doesn't come out.

The boy continues to look for Sounder, but he has no luck. He cries "to fill the vast lostness of the moment." Weeks pass, but there is still no sign of the dog. As Christmas approaches, the boy's mother bakes a cake and asks her son to try to deliver it to his father in jail. He makes the whole trip on foot and is frightened the entire time.

When he gets to town, he must wait in the cold before he is allowed into the jail to see his father. Finally, he is allowed into the jail, but things do not go well for him. The jailer, a "large red-faced man," takes the cake from him: He "squeezed the cake in his hands and broke into four pieces," to make sure no one has hidden a file or hacksaw blade in it. "The boy hated the man with the red face with the same total but helpless hatred he had felt when he saw his father chained." When he does get to see his father, he is sad that he cannot speak from his heart because he is "full of mixed hate and pity." The man asks his son to tell his mother not to grieve and "tell her not to send you no more."

Months pass before Sounder returns, "the living skeleton of what had been a mighty coon hunter." His mighty howl is gone. For several years as soon as crop picking is finished, the boy sets out again to find his father, who has been moved to the county chain gang. His journeys give him a wonderful gift — as he teaches himself to read from the discarded newspapers and magazines he finds in trash barrels. But, once again, when he gets close to his father, he is treated cruelly by a prison guard who throws a chunk of steel at the boy, crushing two of his fingers against the fence.

Although he couldn't find his father, the boy's fortune changes when he stumbled upon a schoolhouse and is befriended by the schoolmaster, who takes it upon himself to help the boy with his schooling. When he returns to tell his mother of his good fortune, she tells him that running into the schoolmaster was a sign from God, and that he should return to study with the man. And so he does, each year in the fall, after he has done his father's work in the field.

One year when the boy is home, Sounder lets out the first howl since his return. The dog runs off down the road to meet the boy's father, who has been released from jail after surviving a near-fatal accident with dynamite while working in the prison quarry. Like Sounder, the man is a ghost of his former self.

One day the boy's father goes out with the dog, but only Sounder returns. When the boy follows the dog, he finds his father lying peacefully in the woods. The boy knows the man is dead. He and his mother bury him. Before the boy sets off to see the schoolmaster, he realizes that Sounder "will be gone before I come home again." He is right. When he returns at Christmas, his mother tells him that the dog "just crawled up under the house and died." The boy is glad, realizing, as he has read in one of his books, "Only the unwise think that what has changed is dead." He knows that his father and his hound will always live in his heart.

CHAPTER ELEVEN

Writing About a Character in a Book

Writing an essay about a character in a book is a lot like writing a report except that instead of taking notes from encyclopedias and magazines, you'll take notes from the novel. You will still write about five or six paragraphs, each one starting with a main idea that is supported in that paragraph with details from the novel. The main difference is where you will get the information that you'll include in your sketch. Instead of taking notes about a real person, you'll take notes about a character you encounter in a novel or a play.

Getting Ideas

The best way to write a sketch about a character in a book is to take notes as you read the book. Yes, it does slow down your reading — not always a bad thing, by the way — but it will give you the details you'll need to support your main ideas about a character. And remember, when brainstorming about a real person, the more good notes you take, the better your chances are of writing a good character sketch.

One way to take notes is to read your novel with your notebook handy. When I take notes while I'm reading, I write the name of a character at the top of a page in my notebook. I like to divide each character page into two columns. I label one column "PHYSICAL" and the other column "PERSONALITY." Then, as I read the novel, I jot down what I notice about the main character. Nothing elaborate. Maybe just a few words about what he looks like or how he acts in a certain situation. In other words, things that will show me what kind of person he is. Because my notes are very brief, I also write down the number of the page on which I found my information. That way I can go back and see how the information fits into a specific point in the whole story. Here are some of my notes from the opening pages of *Stargirl* by Jerry Spinelli:

> p. 4   hair the color of sand, to her shoulders, old
>   wedding dress, carries a ukulele on her back

p. 5	not gorgeous, not ugly, sprinkle of freckles, no makeup
p. 8	red baggy shorts with a bib and shoulder straps
p. 9	singing "Happy Birthday"
p. 10	she wore: flapper dress, kimono, denim miniskirt with green stockings
p. 11	her pet rat in her school bag
pp. 22–23	antics at football game: running around on the field all by herself during halftime

As I am reading the novel and taking notes, I will occasionally stop to read through my notes, looking for connections. For example, I may have jotted down three incidents that show the main character is resourceful or selfish. When I find those kinds of connections, I circle them and draw lines joining them together. For example, take a look at these notes that I circled in my notebook: wears odd clothes, flapper dress, kimono, carries a rat, strums a ukulele, sings "Happy Birthday" to kids she doesn't know, puts a small vase with flowers on her desk, runs around all by herself during halftime at the football game.

I'd circled these notes because they seem related in the way they show eccentric behavior. So, I'd write "ECCENTRIC" on the line that connects these circled notes. If you take a look at my sample report, you'll see that I did, in fact, use those details in a paragraph that began with this sentence: "It's hard to deny that Stargirl is eccentric."

Getting Organized

Finding connections like the ones I noted in the previous paragraph is important when writing about a literary character because the connections are the general ideas that you'll use in the opening sentence of the paragraphs in the body of your sketch. For example, in my sample report,

I wrote a paragraph for each of these opening sentences: "It's hard to deny that Stargirl is eccentric." "Stargirl is always ready to do nice things for people." "In spite of all the wild clothes she wears and the goofy things she does, Stargirl is focused enough to notice things." But, more than anything else, I will remember Stargirl because in the novel she has the courage to stand up for herself. Each sentence is a connection I made in my notes between bits of information that seemed related. Then, when I wrote the paragraphs, I used those bits of information to support each opening sentence.

A good way to organize your notes to see what details you have to support each general trait of a character is to make a chart such as this one:

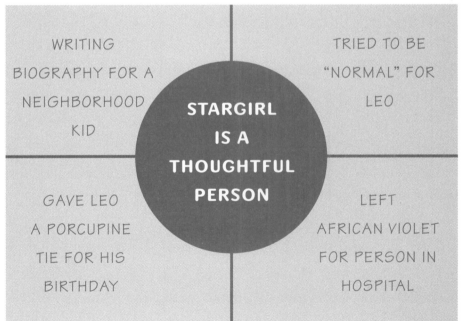

Notice that in the center of the chart I have written a main idea: Stargirl is a thoughtful person. Then, in each of the sections outside of that circle, I have written a detail that supports that main idea. So, in that diagram I have all the basic information — general topic and supporting details — that I need to write one paragraph about Stargirl. If I can do that with two or three other characteristics, I'll be ready to write my draft.

Writing the Draft

If you have drawn up diagrams for each quality that you are going include in the body of your report, writing that part should be a snap. However, you might want to give some extra thought to how you will write your introduction and conclusion.

I think it's a good idea to start a sketch about a character in a book with some sort of personal reaction to the book and/or the character. You'll notice that's the way I started the introduction of my writing model: "We have read lots of books in class this year, and many of their main characters are interesting girls. But I don't think that I've read about a more interesting character than Susan Caraway, a.k.a. Stargirl. Then, in the middle of the paragraph, I use a transitional word — *although* — to shift into the part of the introduction where I mention three things about Stargirl that I will discuss in my essay.

In the conclusion, I complete my essay by expressing why I think she was such an endearing character: "And, even though many of the kids at school had thought of her as 'weird, strange, goofy,' she has the courage to be her own person. And for that reason, Stargirl can be a role model for other girls." I ended on this note because, first of all, I think it's her most important quality. Secondly, the final paragraph in the body of my essay talks about how she has the strength to stand up for herself, which I also mention at the end of my introduction.

The introduction and the conclusion of a character sketch have important functions in a report. The introduction . . . well, it introduces the reader to the subject. It gives a preview of what the reader can expect. And the conclusion . . . well, you guessed it: The conclusion concludes the paper. The essay should sound complete, not simply ended because you ran out of time or couldn't think of anything else to say.

A Word About Craft

Sentence Variety

One way to keep your writing from being boring is to make sure you use a variety of sentence types. You don't want your report to sound like this:

"We have read lots of books in class. Many of them have interesting characters. Stargirl is an interesting character. Many kids think she is weird. She has many good qualities. She helps other people. She is tuned in to the world. She is true to herself."

If you read my writing model, you will see that I included those ideas in a variety of sentences types. Some of my sentences are long. Others are short. Still others are in-between. Some start with the subject. Some start with a clause, like, "Although many of the kids in the book think she is weird, she . . ."

Here are a few sentence types that you can use in your writing:

→ Simple sentence: "The boy in the green shirt left school early."

→ Compound sentence: "He went outside, and his mother picked him up."

→ Complex sentence: "When they got home, he went to sleep."
You can also add a phrase at the beginning of a sentence to make your sentences more interesting:

→ "After I finish my homework, I will watch the ball game."

→ "Failing to get up when the alarm rang, she had to hurry to school."
Try writing some of your sentences in different ways. Combine some sentences. Start some sentences with a phrase. Shorten some sentences that may ramble. Remember that a good piece of writing has many different types of sentences in it.

Revision Checklist

→ Does your writing sound interesting? If not, see what you can do to change sentence structures.

→ Add some variety.

→ Check for transitional words that move your thoughts and ideas from sentence to sentence, from paragraph to paragraph.

→ Have you included enough details from the book to support the main ideas of your report? Look back at your notes if you need more details.

→ Does your introduction mention the main ideas that you will write about in the body of the paper?

→ Does your conclusion end your paper smoothly? Or, do you think your reader might feel that you stopped your paper abruptly?

STARGIRL:

A CHARACTER I'LL NEVER FORGET

by Paul B. Janeczko

Language Arts

Ms. Perez

January 1, 2003

We have read lots of books this year in class, and many of their main characters are interesting girls. But I don't think that I've read about a more interesting character than Susan Caraway, a.k.a. Stargirl, the main character in *Stargirl*, by Jerry Spinelli. Although many of the kids in the book think she is weird, she has many good qualities. She is always ready to help other people. She seems quite tuned in to the world around her. But her most important quality is how she is true to herself.

It is hard to deny that Stargirl is eccentric. Look at the way she dresses at the beginning of the book. In the first month of school she shows up wearing "a 1920s flapper dress. An Indian buckskin. A kimono." And if that isn't enough, one day she wears "a denim miniskirt with green stockings, and crawling up one leg was a parade of enamel ladybug and butterfly pins." And there are all the odd things she does at school. For example, she always carries her pet rat, Cinnamon, around with her. She sings "Happy Birthday" to kids in the cafeteria on their birthdays. She strums a ukulele. She puts a small glass vase on her desk and sticks a flower in it. And who can forget when she cheers for the other team at the basketball games?

Stargirl is always ready to do nice things for people. She gives Leo a porcupine necktie for his birthday but doesn't leave a card with it, so he doesn't know who has left it. When she finds out that someone in a certain house on Marion Drive is in the hospital, she goes to the house and leaves a small African violet with pale violet ribbon tied around the pot. She is writing a biography, complete with snapshots, of a neighborhood kid because she thinks it would be neat if he had all these pictures of himself. Maybe one of the nicest things she does in the novel — even though it doesn't work out well — is the way she changes from Stargirl to a "normal" girl because she doesn't want Leo to feel uncomfortable around her.

In spite of all the wild clothes she wears and the goofy things she does, Stargirl is focused enough to notice things. Not *important* things, just things. Like how the color of the door on a house she passes has been recently painted blue, when it had originally been green. She notices how the old man sitting on a bench at the shopping center holds his hearing aid in his hand and smiles. He wears a small American-flag pin in his lapel. But, as Leo notes, "there was more to her seeing than that. What she saw, she felt. Her eyes went straight to the heart." For example, the old man on the bench makes her cry. Ants struggling with the leg of a beetle make her laugh.

But, more than anything else, I will remember Stargirl because she has the courage to stand up for herself. She does what comes naturally to her, even though the other kids think it is weird. She doesn't care that kids think her clothes are odd. She doesn't care that people stare when she sings "Happy Birthday" to a student she doesn't know very well. The whispering and the silent treatment don't seem to bother her. Not until none of the students are at the school to greet her after she wins the state speech contest. That's when she changes into Susan Caraway and tries to be like everybody else at school. Although Leo is happy with a "normal" girlfriend, Stargirl is miserable because she isn't being true to herself. So, on the night of the Octillo Ball, Stargirl is back, as eccentric as ever, arriving in a sidecar attached to a bicycle driven by her friend Dori and starting a bunny hop line that lasts for hours.

Although Stargirl eventually gives into peer pressure, she is too strong to give in for long. She is so unhappy being Susan that she needs to return to the girl she really is. And, even though many of the kids at school had thought of her as "weird, strange, goofy," she has the courage to be her own person. And for that reason, Stargirl can be a role model for other girls.

CHAPTER TWELVE

Writing a Persuasive Essay

It seems that we can't turn on the television or read a magazine without finding someone who is trying to persuade people to act a certain way. Vote for this candidate. Buy that car. Wear these clothes. But, that's what advertising is all about — trying to convince us to buy something, whether it be a product or a way of life. When you write persuasive essays, you are trying to convince your reader to believe a point of view that you believe. But, if you're going to convince your reader, you'll need information and facts that make for a compelling argument.

Earlier in this book I explained how to write a report about a social issue (see page 99). One of the things I stressed in that section was that your report had to be balanced. In other words, you have to be fair to both sides of the issue, even though you may believe one side very strongly. While it's always a good practice to listen to what others have to say, especially when their opinion differs from yours, when you write an essay to persuade, you are mainly concerned with presenting information that will support your side of the argument. Remember: You are trying to convince the reader of your point of view.

Getting Ideas

If you are the kind of person who has strong opinions, you'll have no problem finding a topic to write about. The problem may come when you need to offer support for your opinion. You'll need good information if you're going to convince someone to believe your side of an issue. Just keep in mind how much you dislike discussions in which someone says to you, "Of course, I'm right. You'll just have to believe me." If you don't want the reader to feel that way about your essay, you'll need to choose a topic that will allow you to present convincing facts to support your point of view.

One way to find a topic for your essay is to look around your school. Are there changes that you'd like to see? Is there an issue that you feel strongly about? Maybe there are people in the school community who feel that the students should wear uniforms. Let's say you think that it's a bad idea. You might want to write an essay that shows why your school does not need such a dress code.

Remember that research need not come from books. You can do personal research. For example, if you are going to write an essay about why the school shouldn't require students to wear uniforms, the first thing you need to do is listen carefully to the people who want kids to wear uniforms. What are their reasons for believing what they do? Once you know their reasons, you can begin your research to challenge their arguments. You might, for instance, know of a school that had required uniforms but went back to letting students wear regular clothes. You might want to visit that school or speak to an administrator on the phone to find out why they didn't keep the uniform dress code. That sort of personal research can be very effective in your essay.

Another way to find a topic is to look at the world around you. Watch the news. Read magazines. Are you in favor of the death penalty? Should SUVs be required to meet the same pollution standards that cars must meet? Should girls be allowed to play football? Find a topic that is real for you, a topic that means something to you. Writing a good essay is hard enough work. Don't make it more difficult by writing about a topic that you're not interested in. Remember: You are trying to persuade someone to listen to your opinion, so put some passion into the process.

You may want to think again about some of the topics you considered for a report on a social issue. You may have listed some interesting topics in your writer's notebook. If not, start a topic list for your persuasive essay. Find a clean page and begin a list of things that concern you. Maybe things that make you angry will find a place on your list. Or, things you've heard about on the news and want to explore further.

Here are some topics that might interest you enough to write an essay:

➡ violence in television and movies and music

➡ gun control

→ school bullies/school violence

→ censorship

→ women in the military

→ child labor and sweatshops

→ the rain forests

→ smokers' rights

→ girls playing on boys' teams/boys playing on girls' teams

→ parental warnings on CDs and music videos

Even if one of these topics doesn't interest you, perhaps there is something in the list that gets you thinking about another subject. As ideas pop into your head, write them down in your writer's notebook.

Taking Notes

Chances are that you're going to write your persuasive issue about a contemporary topic, something that you feel needs attention now. You might choose a topic like gun control, capital punishment, or a dress code at your school. If you take another look at "Writing About a Social Issue," on page 99 of this guide, you'll find some suggestions for doing research in periodicals. The section "Writing a How-To Report" on page 123 gives you some tips on conducting a fruitful personal interview. Another source of good information for your persuasive essay is the Internet. For my sample essay on stopping the use of animals in the circus, for example, I found some compelling information at Web sites that support animal rights. I located these sites by going to a search engine and typing in "animal rights." Then I sifted through the results until I found some sites that supported the position I wanted to take in my sample essay. The next step was to visit those sites and read what they had to offer and take notes. As I mentioned in "Writing About a Social Issue," I recommend printing out information on Web sites (don't forget to include the site URL for anything you download) and taking notes from the hard copy.

That will make it easier for you to underline and highlight worthwhile information.

Getting Organized

A persuasive essay is supposed to convince the reader to consider your point of view on an issue. To help the reader focus on what you are writing, you need to present a logically reasoned argument. To do that, you should organize your essay to have three parts: the introduction, the body, and the conclusion.

The introduction of the essay is meant to "hook" the reader, to get her to want to continue reading. It also prepares the reader for what you are going to present in your essay. In the introduction to my sample essay, I suggest that when we go to a circus, we might be captivated by the clowns and high-wire acts, but we don't often think how the "wild" animals in the circus are trained to perform. I end the introduction with a strong statement that makes clear how I feel about such training: "It's time that we outlaw animals in the circus."

The body of your essay will probably have three paragraphs to it, one for each point that you're trying to make. There's nothing magic about having three parts in the body of your paper. You could have more, although making only two points in your essay might not be very convincing. Each point, in turn, will be supported by your evidence, the specific details that you have obtained from research. All this might seem complicated, but it's not. And it does give you an easy way to organize your material.

I'd suggest that you use one page of your notebook for each of the main points that you will cover in the body of your essay. Draw a line down the center of each page. At the top of the page, write the point you'd like to make in the paragraph. For example, one of the main points in my writing model is that training is also a horror these wild animals must endure. In the left-hand column, write down the support you have for that point, then use the right-hand column to write down where you got that information. Here's something else that I would write in the left-hand column on another page: "Travel can be a horrible experience for circus animals." In the right-hand column I would note that I found that information at the Web site of the People for the Ethical Treatment of Animals.

Organizing this way does a couple of things to help you write a good essay. First of all, it gives you the chance to write down the main ideas for your essay. It also gives you the chance to note how you will support each main idea. Finally, it will also give you the space to write down the source of your information.

Research Tip

Looking at Subheadings

Did you ever notice when you read through an encyclopedia entry or an article on a Web site that it frequently has subheadings sprinkled throughout the text? They're usually in bold type to set them off from the rest of the text. They're meant to get your attention and to alert you to what will be in the sections that follow. Although you may rush through these breaks in the text without giving them too much attention, they can be valuable tools to you as a reader and a researcher. These subheadings can help give you a clue about the contents of the section — maybe a paragraph or two — that you are about to read. If you keep that topic in mind, it can help you focus as you read.

The subheadings can also help you as a researcher. Taken together, those subheadings offer a brief outline of the main points that will be covered in the article. They can also suggest topics that you might want to use in your research or your essay topic.

For example, when I was doing research for my writing model on the treatment of circus animals, I found that most of the articles I read mentioned six topics:

1. travel
2. training
3. public safety
4. educational value
5. performances
6. animal conservation

Although I was keeping my eyes open for anything related to my topic, most of the notes I took fell into these six main categories.

Once I had taken my notes, I realized that I had far too much material for a short essay. Because I wanted the strongest arguments to support my opinion, I found the most valuable information at Web sites created by organizations like the Humane Society International, People for the Ethical Treatment of Animals, and Captive Animals Protective Society. However, I needed to decide which were the most important categories. One way to decide this is to see in which categories you have the most notes. Another way is to go with the categories that mean the most to you. That's what I decided to do and wound up with four main parts to my essay: travel, training, educational value, and conservation. You'll see that they make up the main parts of the outline for my essay.

Writing the Draft

If you carefully build the paragraphs in the body of your essay — starting with a topic sentence that expresses the main idea of the paragraph and following it with information and facts that will support that idea — you will wind up with a good essay. So, as you draft each paragraph, give some thought to what you will say in your topic sentence. Your topic sentence should be a general statement that you can support in the paragraph with clear and specific information from your research.

Take another look at the topic sentence I mentioned above: "Travel can be a horrible experience for circus animals." That is a general statement that needs support. I use the rest of the paragraph to support that topic sentence. Notice how the following sentence is too narrow and factual to be a good topic sentence: "When they travel, the animals are deprived of their social life that is so important in the wild." Here's a topic sentence that is an opinion that would be hard to support with facts: "I think it's stupid to hurt circus animals." So, when you write the topic sentences of the paragraphs in the body of a persuasive essay, make sure that (a) they are general statements that can be supported with details, and (b) that you have the information to back them up.

A Word About Craft

Tone

One thing that needs your attention when you write a persuasive essay is the tone. Since you are trying to get your readers to listen to your opinion on a topic, make sure that you do not offend them by belittling them or otherwise insulting them. Avoid making demeaning statements like, "Anyone with half a brain can see that . . ." or "Only a fool would not believe what I believe." In other words, show your reader the same kind of respect that you'd like to be shown.

At the same time, you must guard against patronizing your readers by not giving them credit for knowing certain things. They may not know as much about the subject of your essay as you do, especially if you are writing about a subject that is a passion for you. However, you want to make sure that you don't show off your knowledge with statements like, "As just about everybody knows . . ." As you write your essay, put yourself in the place of the reader. Pretend that you have not given much thought to the subject. Or, that you feel differently about the subject. Ask yourself, How would this essay make me feel? If you feel that the writer gives you credit for being able to think and make decisions, then your essay probably has the proper tone.

Revision Checklist

→ Have you supported your main ideas with solid information? Do you need to add more supporting details?

→ Can you follow the logical flow of the paragraph or do you need to rearrange some of the paragraphs?

→ Since you're trying to convince someone of your point of view, have you addressed the reader in a respectful tone?

→ Do all your sentences and paragraphs work together to make a convincing argument? Do you weaken your argument by including some information that doesn't help?

→ How do your sentences sound? Do many of them sound the same? Can you restructure a few sentences to make the essay sound less monotonous?

THE CRUELEST SHOW ON EARTH?

by Paul B. Janeczko

Language Arts

Ms. Perez

January 1, 2003

OUTLINE

I. Introduction.

II. Travel can be a horrible experience.

    A. Many hours on the road.

    B. Travel in extreme weather.

    C. Confined to "beast wagons."

    D. Deprived of socialization.

III. Training is often a horror.

A. Takes place behind closed doors.

B. Animals are frequently beaten.

C. Animal-rights advocates are not allowed to observe training.

IV. Not an educational experience.

A. Animals kept in unnatural environments.

B. Made to perform unnatural tricks.

C. We are better off watching animals filmed in the wild.

V. Not serving conservation cause.

A. Many animals are not bred in captivity.

B. Animals are frequently taken from the wild.

C. Some circuses have tried to traffic in endangered species.

VI. Conclusion.

· ·

THE CRUELEST SHOW ON EARTH?

When most of us hear the word *circus*, we think of clowns, high-wire acts, and wild animals. However, what many of us don't realize is that behind the excitement and glitter of the Greatest Show on Earth there is a dark side that the circus keeps secret. That is the world of abuse that circus animals must endure in the name of entertainment. It's time that we outlaw animals in the circus.

Travel can be a horrible experience for circus animals. Because the circus visits so many cities in all kinds of weather — some travel thousands of miles and are on the road for as long as forty-eight weeks per year (Defense) — circus animals are crowded into beast wagons that are often too small for them. Frequently they travel through extreme weather. The animals are deprived of their social life that is so important in the wild. Elephants, for example, spend almost the entire day barely able to move (HSI).

Training is also a horror that these wild animals must endure. All training takes place behind closed doors. It can be brutal. Animals are often beaten and abused as part of their training (CAPS). Standard practice is to beat, shock, and whip the animals to make them perform their ridiculous tricks (PETA). When the circus allows animal-rights organizations to observe training, they are really only allowed to see rehearsals, not the training process (CAPS).

Circus people want us to believe that performing animals present an educational experience for customers, but this is not true. Animals are kept in an unnatural environment and made to perform unnatural tricks (CAPS). Animals will run and jump in the wild if they want to, but elephants do not stand on their heads and horses do not walk on their hind legs in the wild. If we want to learn about animals, we are better off watching a wild-animal show that *was* filmed in the wild (CAPS).

Many people believe that the circus performs a valuable conservation duty by breeding animals in captivity. A look at the facts shows otherwise. Many animals we see performing in the circus were taken from the wild. Elephant calves that wind up in the circus, for example, are often the survivors of culls, which are really the mass slaughter of adult elephants (CAPS). And, not too long ago, some African traveling circuses were suspected of being "fronts for trafficking in endangered species" (*Earth* p. 14), like parrots and chimpanzees.

The next time the circus rolls into town, don't be blind to what is really going on under the big top. The circus is more than clowns and acrobats. It is a showcase for animals that are severely mistreated—animals that are denied the opportunity to live dignified lives, running free with their species. When the circus comes to town, just say, No!

BIBLIOGRAPHY

Captive Animals Protective Society (CAPS) Web site. www.captiveanimlas.org, February 2, 2002.

Earth Island Journal. Fall 1997, p. 14.

Humane Society International of Australia Web site. www.hsi.org.au/circus, February 2, 2002.

In Defense of Animals Web site. www.idausa.org, February 2, 2002.

People for the Ethical Treatment of Animals (PETA) Web site link. www.circuses.com, February 2, 2002.

CHAPTER THIRTEEN

Writing a Problem-Solution Essay

in 1969 as the brainchild
anted to open a recordi
llage in upstate New Yo
3ob Dylan. The businessm
attract a lot of attention
metown. Although they h
s to risk money on t
estors were interested
of this project that was
Music and Art F
Days of Peace a
accommodate
end the fair, t
was move
nsidered wh
assing any "m
lence" (American
peace singers like
her acts were soon
formers read like a
luding the Grateful
arwater Revival, and
o took pains to plan f
ilities, and a medical st
t went into Woodstoc

You could say that the problem-solution essay takes the persuasive essay and carries it one step further. And that step is where you offer some sort of solution to the problem that you describe in the first part of your essay. This means that you will need to research possible solutions to include in your essay. You're not likely to find the perfect solution to your issue, but you are apt to find a number of possible ways to lessen a problem. And, just as you need to make sure that your persuasive essay is convincing, you'll need to include convincing solutions to the problem.

Getting Ideas

Writing a problem-solution essay is a great way to get involved with the community in which you live or go to school. For example, if you see that the neighborhood ball field is in horrible shape — overgrown weeds, dilapidated bleachers, broken outfield fence — you might be able to offer some solutions to that problem. Or, if you don't like the way a certain segment of the student body is treated, you might be able to offer some suggestions on how that problem can be addressed.

If you take on a community problem in your essay, the solution might be what some people need to do to make a change. It could be, for example, that the student body is not aware of the mistreatment of some students. It's possible that your essay, read at a class meeting or written as a letter to your school newspaper, could get the wheels of change rolling. So, be aware of what's going on in your community. You might be able to change things for the better. And get a good grade on your essay!

Getting Organized

Because this is a two-part essay — the problem and the solution — you'll want to organize your thoughts to show the connection between both parts. To see this connection, write various aspects of your problem on one page of your notebook, then write your solutions on the facing page. There need not be a strict connection between one aspect of the problem and one solution, although there might be. For example, here are

some of the notes I jotted down when I was trying to organize my problem-solution writing model:

PROBLEM			SOLUTION
-Travel can be horrible	○	○	-Ask sponsors to support
			animal-free circuses
-Training is often cruel			-Write a letter to the editor
-Not an educational			-Organize a demonstration
experience	○	○	-Contact a state legislator
-Not serving conservation			-Stay informed

You can see that there is not a direct connection between each aspect
of the problem and the solutions. Rather, my solutions are directed at the
overall issue of mistreatment of circus animals.

Taking Notes

When I was doing the research for "The Cruelest Show on Earth?," my
sample essay in the previous chapter, I discovered that most of the Web
sites I checked for information about the mistreatment of circus animals
offered solutions to the problem. These sites made it easy for me to suggest a solution to the problem that I was writing about.

I mention this because it might help you when it comes time to select
a topic for your problem-solution essay to choose a problem for which
you can find solutions as you do your research, whether in be online or
in periodicals and books. Of course, you can always modify the solutions
suggested in your research and come up with your own solutions.

Writing the Draft

As you read the following writing model, you will notice that the bulk of
it is the same as "The Cruelest Show on Earth?," my persuasive essay.
However, I changed the last sentence of my original conclusion so that
the paragraph now serves as a transition into the solution part of the
essay. Then, I wrote a new conclusion to wrap up my problem-solution

essay. My outline is changed to include the solution part of the essay, but my bibliography remained the same because I was able to find suggestions for solutions from the same sources that discussed the problem.

As you write the solution part of the report, remember to be reasonable in what you offer as a solution to a problem. If you want your suggestions to be taken seriously, they must be things that your reader might actually be able to do. So, I didn't suggest, for instance, that the readers chain themselves to a tiger's cage or go on a hunger strike until the elephants are let loose! Obviously, these suggestions are too far-fetched for most readers to take seriously. But that's not to say that your solution must be something that takes no effort. The effort you expect, however, must be reasonable.

Make sure you offer three or four suggestions rather than one sweeping quick-fix solution. You want to give your readers a few choices of things they can do to help lessen the problem, because some people are comfortable doing some things that would make other people uneasy. For example, you might write a letter to the editor about a problem, but you would feel uncomfortable speaking to someone in your state legislature about that problem.

A Word About Craft

Active and Passive Voices

Good writing is lively writing. One of the best ways to make your writing lively is to use the active voice, rather than the passive voice, as much as possible. In an active voice sentence, the subject of the sentence is doing the action, as in, "The second baseman booted the ball." In this sentence, the second baseman is performing the action of the sentence. In a passive voice sentence, the subject of the sentence is having the action done to it, as in, "The ball was booted by the second baseman." Can you see how the ball is receiving the action? Because you need to include helping verbs in passive voice sentences, the sentences are automatically longer than active voice sentences. But, more than that, they are simply not as lively as direct active-voice sentences. Because active voice is more direct, it is a more forceful way of writing. It is also more convincing writing, which helps the writer persuade the reader.

Here are some passive voice sentences that have been revised and written in the active voice. Notice the difference.

→ Passive: A delicious turkey was cooked by Mom for the Sunday luncheon.

→ Active: Mom baked a delicious turkey for the Sunday luncheon.

→ Passive: All the details were taken by the police officer.

→ Active: The police officer took all the details.

→ Passive: The book was written by my friend.

→ Active: My friend wrote the book.

→ Passive: A shoe was lost by someone at the movies.

→ Active: Someone at the movies lost a shoe.

Revision Checklist

→ Have you minimized your use of passive voice sentences? Before you hand in your final copy, see if you can change passive voice sentences to active voice sentences.

→ Do any of your ideas seem out of place? Would it help to move them to a different part of the essay?

→ Are the solutions that you offer reasonable?

→ Have you written the problem and solution parts of this essay with an appropriate tone?

YOU CAN HELP STOP CRUELTY

TO CIRCUS ANIMALS:

A PROBLEM-SOLUTION REPORT

by Paul B. Janeczko

Language Arts Class

Ms. Perez

January 1, 2003

OUTLINE

I. Introduction.

II. Travel can be a horrible experience.

    A. Many hours on the road.

    B. Travel in extreme weather.

    C. Confined to "beast wagons."

    D. Deprived of socialization.

III. Training is often a horror.

    A. Takes place behind closed doors.

    B. Animals are frequently beaten.

    C. Animal-rights advocates are not allowed to observe training.

IV. Not an educational experience.

    A. Animals kept in unnatural environments.

    B. Made to perform unnatural tricks.

    C. We are better off watching animals filmed in the wild.

V. Not serving conservation cause.

    A. Many animals are not bred in captivity.

    B. Animals are frequently taken from the wild.

    C. Some circuses have tried to traffic in
       endangered species.

VI. There are some things you can do.

    A. Ask sponsors to support animal-free circuses.

    B. Write a letter to the editor.

VII. Get some adults to help.

    A. Organize a demonstration at the circus.

    B. Contact a state legislator.

VIII. Stay informed.

    A. Read as much as you can about the issue.

    B. Get information from animal-rights Web sites.

IX. Conclusion.

- -

YOU CAN HELP STOP CRUELTY TO CIRCUS ANIMALS:
A PROBLEM-SOLUTION ESSAY

When most of us hear the word *circus*, we think of clowns, high-wire acts, and wild animals. However, what many of us don't realize is that behind the excitement and glitter of the Greatest Show on Earth there is a dark side that the circus keeps secret. That is the world of abuse that circus animals must endure in the name of entertainment. And it's time that we outlaw animals in the circus.

Travel can be a horrible experience for circus animals. Because the circus visits so many cities in all kinds of weather — some travel thousands of miles for as long as forty-eight weeks per year (Defense) — circus animals are crowded into beast wagons that are often too small for them. Often they travel through extreme weather. The animals are deprived of their social life that is so important in the wild. Elephants, for example, spend almost the entire day barely able to move (HSI).

Training is also a horror that these wild animals must endure. All training takes place behind closed doors. It is often brutal. Animals are often beaten and abused as part of their training (CAPS). Standard practice is to beat, shock, and whip the animals to make them perform their ridiculous tricks (PETA). When the circus allows animal-rights organizations to observe training, they are really only allowed to see rehearsals, not the training process (CAPS).

Circus people want us to believe that performing animals present an educational experience for customers, but this is not true. Animals are kept in an unnatural environment and made to perform unnatural tricks (CAPS). Animals will run and jump in the wild if they want to, but elephants do not stand on their heads and horses do not walk on their hind legs in the wild. If we want to learn about animals, we are betting off watching a wild-animal show that *was* filmed in the wild (CAPS).

Many people believe that the circus performs a valuable conservation duty by breeding animals in captivity. A look at the facts shows otherwise. Many animals we see performing in the circus were taken from the wild. Elephant calves, for example, are often the survivors of culls, which are really mass slaughter of adult elephants that are sold to circuses (CAPS). And, not too long ago, some African traveling circuses were suspected of being "fronts for trafficking in endangered species" (*Earth* p. 14), like parrots and chimpanzees.

The next time the circus rolls into town, don't be blind to what is really going on under the big top. The circus is more than clowns and acrobats. It is a showcase for animals that are severely mistreated—animals that are denied the opportunity to live dignified lives, running free with their species. But you shouldn't feel powerless to help the animals. You can take action to stop the cruelty.

There are a number of things you can do to help circus animals. First of all, try to get the show canceled. You can get in touch with the local sponsors and ask them to support animal-free circuses, like Cirque du Soleil, The New Pickle Family Circus, and Circus Ingenieux. You can also write a letter to the editor of the local newspaper, explaining how the animals are mistreated. You can even get some of your classmates to sign the letter before you mail it.

If you can get some adults interested in the issue of animal cruelty, they might be able to help you organize a peaceful protest of the circus. You might even be able to hand out information sheets that explain the issue. Of course, you would need to check the local laws about such a demonstration. You might also contact your local legislator of the state government and discuss the possibility of passing a law that would prohibit circuses with exotic animals.

While you are trying to stop cruelty to circus animals, you must do your best to stay informed about the issue. Read as much about the problem as you can. A good place to start is at the Web sites of these animal-rights organizations:

- People for the Ethical Treatment of Animals (PETA): www.circuses.com
- Performing Animals Welfare Society (PAWS): www.pawsweb.org
- In Defense of Animals: www.idausa.org
- National Animals Interest Alliance: www.naiaonline.org

Always remember that these mistreated animals cannot speak for themselves. They need concerned people to do their talking. You can be one of those people. Learn more about the issue and do whatever you can to help.

BIBLIOGRAPHY

Captive Animals Protective Society (CAPS) Web site. www.captiveanimlas.org, February 2, 2002.

Earth Island Journal. Fall 1997, p. 14.

Humane Society International of Australia Web site. www.hsi.org.au/circus, February 2, 2002.

In Defense of Animals Web site. www.idausa.org, February 2, 2002.

People for the Ethical Treatment of Animals Web site link. www.circuses.com, February 2, 2002.

CHAPTER FOURTEEN

Writing About Yourself

f you're like most of the young people I meet when I visit schools to talk about writing, you probably think your life is dull, that nothing exciting ever happened to you (and never will!), that you've never met anyone interesting, that no one in the world would care to read anything you had to say about your life. While some of that might be true, if you take the time to examine your life, I suspect that you'll be surprised by what you come to realize about it. Oh, your life might never make the six o'clock news or the cover of a supermarket tabloid (lucky you!), but I'm willing to bet that your life is richer than you think.

You might be asking yourself, "Even if I could find something interesting in my life, why should I bother to write it?" If you never show a soul a single word of what you write about yourself, there are benefits to doing such writing. Whether you write about yourself in a journal, in an e-mail to a friend, or for an assignment for school, you will be richer for the experience.

The most important reason to write about your life is to help you discover the answer to the question that folks have been asking for hundreds of years: Who am I? It's a great question, although the answers aren't always easy to find or pleasant to face. Nevertheless, if you're lucky, it is a question that you will be asking yourself for the rest of your life. I say "if you're lucky" because asking that question is a great way to learn more about yourself. The answers to that question — and there will be many answers because you are a complex person, believe it or not — will be changing because you'll be changing in some pretty interesting ways. By writing about yourself, you'll be learning more about yourself and that will help you grow. And the more you examine your life — the good as well as the not-so-good parts — the richer it will become.

Another reason for writing about your life is that it may give you a chance to heal old wounds and clarify misunderstandings. For example, if you think you were wronged by a friend — maybe you heard that she was spreading untrue rumors about you — writing about that incident may give you the chance to see what she did in a different light. You might be able to better understand why she did that — was she jealous of your popularity at school? — and bring yourself to forgive her, or at least let go of that hurt. And you might learn something that will help you in dealing with friends. For example, that it's never okay to spread rumors, even if you are jealous.

Getting Ideas

Before you can write about your life, you need to take a good look at it, think about it, and write some notes about it. Those notes and scribblings will be just like the paint an artist uses to create a portrait. The better your notes, the better your chances of finding some material that would make for an interesting piece of autobiographical writing. And, just as an artist keeps her material in a paint box, you will use your writer's notebook to keep the notes of your life. Let me suggest topics you can write about in your notebook to help you discover rich material to include in your autobiographical writing.

A word of caution before you start working with these activities. I hope that most of the memories that come into your mind are pleasant ones. However, not all the memories will be happy because our lives are a blend of happy and sad memories. If you find that some of the memories are too difficult for you to deal with, stop working with them. Try a different activity. However, if the memory is unhappy but not horrible, try to stick with it because you may grow as a person when you face a memory and write about it. Sometimes just writing an unhappy memory is enough to take away its hurt. But don't be afraid or ashamed if you need to speak to an adult you trust if an unpleasant memory stays on your mind.

→ Time Line

A good way to start gathering material about your life is to get "the big picture." In other words, take a look at your whole life. You can do that by drawing a time line of your life. To make sure that your time line isn't too cramped, give yourself two facing pages of your notebook. Across the top of both pages, write in bold letters: **TIME LINE OF MY LIFE**. Now, at a point about a third of the way down the left-hand page write the year of your birth. From that point draw a horizontal line to the edge of the other page. Now, about two thirds of the way down the page, draw a line that is parallel to the one you just drew. Stop that line about an inch before the edge of the right-hand page. In that inch space, write in the current year. Your time line should look like this:

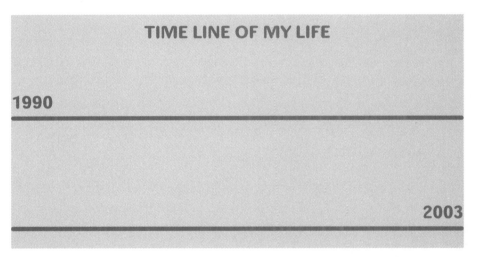

TIME LINE OF MY LIFE

1990

2003

The purpose of the time line is to give you a place to record the important points of your life so far. Some people call the most important events in their lives "stepping stones," as you move from one point in your life to a new point. Sometimes the events will be dramatic: a relative's death, your family moving to a new state across the country, your enrollment in a new school. Other events will be less spectacular but no less important to you: You learned how to ride a two wheeler, you won a blue ribbon at the fair, you went to your first major-league baseball game. Those sorts of events deserve a spot on the time line of your life.

When you think of an event that you want to include on your time line, draw a small vertical line through the time line, then write the year below the line and the event above the line. As you put more items on your time line, it will look something like this:

TIME LINE OF MY LIFE

1990	1995	1996	1997	1998
	KINDERGARTEN	1ST GRADE	MOVED TO NJ	FLEW TO VISIT GRANDMA

1999	2000	2001	2002	2003
NEW BEST FRIEND: AMY	STARTED GIRLSCOUTS 1ST CAMP IN SUMMER	NEW BIKE & ROLLER BLADES FOR BIRTHDAY	PLAYED 1ST SOCCER GAME	

One of the good things about the time line is that you can keep adding to it as you think of other events that are important to your life. In other words, you don't need to finish your time line in one sitting. You might create a good time line but then, maybe at a family party, your aunt mentions something that happened to you that you had completely forgotten about. You can easily add that to your time. If it gets too crowded, copy it over on a larger sheet of paper or move on to another two-page spread in your journal, but draw in three lines rather than the two that I suggested.

Let me offer one more suggestion for working with the time line. As you work on it and recall an event or a person, go to a fresh page in your notebook and jot down some notes about that subject—the first things that come to mind. Don't stop to think about what you are writing. Just write it all down. You can fiddle with it later and see if you can turn those notes into a personal narrative.

→ Neighborhood Map

Can you think of the best neighborhood you have lived in? It might be the neighborhood you live in now. Or perhaps the neighborhood you lived in a few years ago is still special to you. It doesn't matter which neighborhood you choose.

Close your eyes. Imagine that you are magically hovering over that neighborhood that you liked so much. What do you see down there? Keep your eyes closed but use your memory to notice what is in the streets and in the backyards. What buildings do you see? What are the names of the people who live in the houses? What are the names of the streets? Are there fences? Trees? Abandoned buildings? Woods? Empty lots? Stores? Picture the whole neighborhood. Don't overlook the small details. Keep your eyes closed for another few minutes as you take your time to get a bird's-eye view of the neighborhood.

When you open your eyes, draw a map of that neighborhood. No, don't put if off until later. You'll lose your memory view. Neatness doesn't count, so don't slave over making the streets perfectly straight or the houses evenly spaced. Your map must, however, be neat enough for you to read easily. Graph paper might help you. Write in all the names you can remember: streets, people, stores, schools, churches. Take your time adding details. You might be surprised at the things you remember and notice from that neighborhood. No detail is too small to put on your map.

When you think your neighborhood map is complete, study it and see what stories come from the map. Maybe a neighbor's name reminds you of a Halloween prank you played with your friends. Maybe the woods behind the houses were where you and your friends built a tree house in which you had hours of fun. On another page in your notebook, take notes about anything you remember. Perhaps one of these ideas will turn into a personal narrative.

→ House or Apartment Floor Plan

Making a floor plan of the house you grew up in (or the house that you currently live in) is another way to recall some of the things that happened to you. If you draw a plan of your current house, you have an advantage because you can simply walk around the house, mapping it as you go. If you're drawing a plan for a house you used to live in, you should try to close your eyes as you did with the neighborhood map you drew and let your memory take over. Imagine yourself in that house again, walking from room to room, drawing in all the furniture that you remember.

When you have finished drawing your floor plan, let your memory walk through the door that you usually use. Slowly walk from room to room, jotting down along the edges of the plan any memories that your walk brings up. You may remember the room where the Christmas tree was set up, which may trigger some holiday memories. You may remember the time you made breakfast in bed for your parents and everything turned out delicious. Or maybe by the back door is where you dumped your sports equipment when you came in from practice, which may remind you of the time you scored the winning goal in the championship hockey game.

Don't overlook small details. They might seem insignificant, but they could, in fact, turn out to be the key to writing about an important experience in your life. Take your time with your floor plan. There's no rush to finish it. And, like the neighborhood map, it is the kind of thing that you can come back to from time to time when a new "house memory" sparks in your mind.

➜ Hair Autobiography

You're right: Nobody would really be interested in reading the life of your hair. However, making a list of the ways you've worn your hair might just give you some ideas for your personal writing. So, make a list of the way you've worn your hair over the years. You could make it like a chart, with the type of hairstyle followed by the year you wore that style. Or you could make this list like another time line.

How is your hairstyle in fourth grade going to help you write about yourself? Well, when you think of that hair style and that grade in school, it might remind you of other things that happened around that time. For instance, maybe that hairstyle reminds you of how difficult it was for you to adjust to a new school after your family moved. Or maybe when you were getting your hair cut, you met another kid and you became friends. So, the style of your hair is not important. What might be important is any connections that the hairstyle recalls for you.

If you're like me and don't pay a lot of attention to your hair or its style, you might want to write a brief autobiography in relationship to

➜ houses you've lived in

➜ pets you've had

➜ your friends

➜ family vacations

➜ holidays and celebrations

➜ birthdays parties

➜ schools you've attended

➜ injuries you've suffered

Remember as you write that the important parts are the associations you make with the people, places, and things in your life's story. Don't be surprised if some lists are more fruitful than others. For example, when you write your autobiography in terms of family vacations, you might find many more things to write about than when you write about the pets you've had.

➜ Treasure Chest

Even though you've probably never sailed the seven seas in search of buried treasures, I wouldn't be surprised if you have a treasure chest buried someplace in your room. I know I do. I'm talking about that place where you stash all those important souvenirs and reminders of the great things that have happened to you. Your treasures might be in a shoe box stashed in the back of your closet or under your bed. Maybe you have a drawer in your bureau where you keep your most important mementos.

If you don't have a treasure chest, why don't you think of starting one? You could decorate the chest by cutting out pictures from magazines that show your interests. Look around your room for things that deserve a place of honor in your treasure chest. Check in your closet. In your bureau drawers. As you put things in your treasure chest, see if any of them spark memories that are worth saving and sharing with someone else in a personal narrative. Don't forget that you can also keep your personal writing private in your journal.

➜ Family Tree

In many cases, our memories are tied to people in our family. Brothers and sisters, maybe, and parents, of course, but also, perhaps, an aunt or a grandfather. You might remember when an aunt took you into the city to see a play. Maybe your grandfather taught you how to ride a bike. If you take the time to think about it, you might be surprised how many of your memories are tied to members of your immediate family as well as to your extended family.

Create a family tree. My family tree would look like this:

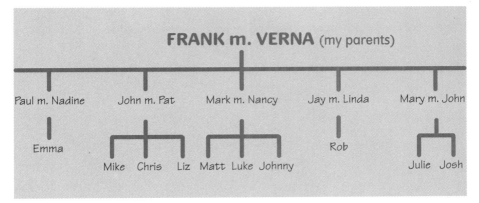

I suggest you begin your family tree as I have, with your immediate family, because you know that part of your family best. Then branch out from your mother and your father. See how far you can go. Ask your parents for some help if you are unsure about some of your aunts and uncles and distant cousins.

As you work on your family tree, jot down any memories that come to mind. If you are lucky, you'll find a memory or two that would make a compelling story.

→ Life Map

You've already made a map of your neighborhood and a floor plan of a home you lived in. Now, make a map of where you have been in your life. If you have traveled a lot, perhaps with a parent who was in the military or on family vacations, you might want to photocopy a map of the United States as the basis for your life map. If you've stayed pretty close to home, you can still draw a life map. It will simply be on a more limited scale, perhaps of the state you live in or even city you live in.

Once you decide on the map you are going to use for your life map — whether it is a photocopy or a drawn map doesn't matter — start to mark up the map with the events of your life. You can draw a star on the spot where something important happened, then shoot a line from the star to the margin and write a quick note that explains that spot. If you don't have room on the map for arrows and notes in the margin, you can number each important spot and write an explanation of each number in your notebook. Be on the lookout for ideas that will make good topics for autobiographical writing.

→ Life Lists

I'm a great list-maker. My desk and bureau are blanketed with small scraps of papers with two or three things scribbled on each: books I want to read (or reread), friends I need to be in touch with, chores around the house I need to do, or maybe even a list of words that I like. Lists are a great way to organize things. And, who knows, if you pay close attention when you write some of these lists, you may find a long list of topics for personal narratives.

Here are a few suggestions for writing your own life lists:

→ your childhood heroes and heroines, both real people and people you read about or saw in movies and on TV

→ a "brag list," things you're good at

→ ways you have changed and why you changed

→ ten people you would like to meet in your life

→ things that people could say about you that would make you feel good

Another idea that might help is to keep a few pages of your notebook strictly for your memories. You might write "I REMEMBER . . ." at the top of a page and, quite simply, write down things that you remember. They could be things from last week or last year. Or they might be things that you had forgotten until your little brother started talking about how much he wants a pet, which got you thinking about a pet you once had. Write about it in your notebook. Of course, you won't write a personal narrative about all the remembered things you jot down. But, if you don't jot stuff down, you'll never know what you're missing.

The more you explore your past, the more you'll find things that you can write about. You might, for instance, see a connection between two events that happened some time apart. You might see something like a theme in your life as a kid. For example, you may have been very lucky to have lots of wonderful friends. Or you might have had nothing but bad luck when it came to pets. So, as you take notes and read them over, be on the lookout for connections. Use highlighters to show these connections, or draw lines and arrows to show them.

Talking with Family Members

Research Tip

Just because these activities are designed to help you write about your life, don't be afraid to get some help as you take notes in your notebook. If you look through family scrapbooks or photo albums (or those boxes of photos in the back of the hall closet), I'll bet that you will find a lot of pictures that will jog your memory. Talk to your parents to get other ideas. Maybe you can look through family photographs with them. I suspect they will get as big a kick out of a trip down memory lane as you do. Ask questions. What kind of kid were you? What things about you do your parents remember? But don't stop with your parents. Write letters or send e-mails to other relatives and ask them what memories of you they might have. (If nothing else, it's a good way to keep in touch with your relatives.)

Getting Organized

All the lists of ideas in the world will not guarantee that you'll write a good personal narrative. To do that, you must develop your ideas, organize them, and write them clearly. But, it all starts with a memorable event in your life that you would like to share with others.

Let's suppose that I want to write about an incident that happened to me and one of my younger brothers around Christmas many years ago. How do I start? The first thing I would do is write down the basic facts of the story. A good way to get the basic facts down on paper is to draw a circle that fills a page of your notebook. Divide the circle into six equal wedges. Next to each section, write one of these headings: Who? What? Where? When? Why? How did I feel? Answering those six questions will give you the basic information you need to write your narrative. For my story, it would look like this:

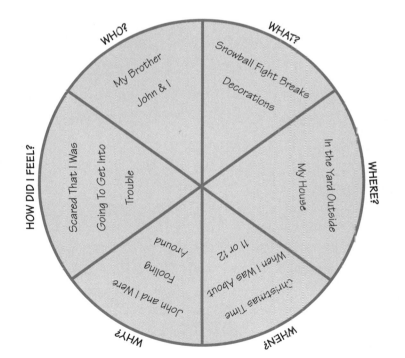

Keeping Related Words Together

One of the ways to write clearly is to keep related words together in a sentence. You don't want to separate the subject and the verb with a clause or phrase. Also, make sure that you keep clauses and phrases close to the words they modify. Here are some examples:

1. As a student, if she doesn't do her homework, will receive poor grades. Revised: If a student doesn't do her homework, she will receive poor grades.

2. My mother, when she got out of the car, slipped on the ice.
   Revised: When my mother got out of the car, she slipped on the ice.

3. My brother visited me who lives in Los Angeles.
   Revised: My brother, who lives in Los Angeles, visited me.

4. Sleeping under the car, I spotted Sally's pet ferret.
   Revised: I spotted Sally's pet ferret sleeping under the car.

Writing the Draft

When I have a pile of information and memories for my narrative written out in my notebook, I'm ready to start drafting. As I work on the draft, I'll try to be aware of spots where I can add sense details to make the piece of writing come alive: things, sounds, smells, physical details. Because my brother John and I exchanged some words, I will try to include those in the dialogue of my narrative. I can't remember exactly what we said those many years ago, but I can remember a few things we did say, and I can add other bits of dialogue that seem probable. I want to make sure that it is clear what I was thinking and how I was feeling during this escapade of ours. And I don't have to worry about paragraphs. Not in my draft. I just write.

This personal narrative is a straightforward story told in chronological order. That's the easiest and most common way to tell a story. But, when you start drafting, remember that you cannot include *everything* in your narrative, even though it might be about a very brief incident in your life. The story of my brother and me took less than an hour of our lives. But I want to include enough details to give the reader a clear sense of what happened. If you cram in too many details that are not really important to the story you're trying to tell, the story may get boring. For example, at the time of the story I'm going to write, our family owned a blue and white Ford station wagon, with a white interior and automatic transmission. Those are facts. But they add nothing to my story, so I need to resist putting them in just because I am so proud of myself for remembering them.

Another thing to remember as you write your draft is to let yourself be open to surprise. What I mean is that, even though you think you know exactly what happened in your story, writing it all down could very well bring up things that you'd forgotten. Also, the passing of time might allow you to look at the incident with new eyes. In other words, be open to new discoveries in some old territory.

Revision Checklist

➡ Do you keep related words in your sentences close together?

➡ Do you use appropriate transitional words to allow your reader to easily follow your narrative?

➡ Does your narrative sound complete? Do you think it could be improved with more details?

➡ Does your story contain information that does not really help the story?

PERSONAL NARRATIVE:

THE SNOWBALL FIGHT

by Paul B. Janeczko

Language Arts

Ms. Perez

November 6, 2001

The house vibrated with Christmas spirit. At least it did for my brother John and me. We were on Christmas vacation, we had no homework, and the ground was covered with snow. For my parents it was a different matter because they were busy with last-minute cleaning and cooking for the party that would bring a dozen relatives to our house in a couple of hours. My father, never much of a party guy, wasn't looking forward to the relatives. My mother, wanting to have everything "just right," was getting frantic. That explained why she threw John and me out of the house.

"Just go outside," she said. "You're getting in the way."

John started to protest, but she cut him off by saying, "It's okay. Just go. Your father and I will finish up."

So, out the door we went, after pulling knit-wool caps on our heads, slipping on jackets and gloves, and wrapping scarves around our necks.

The air was calm but crisp. Although it was only four o'clock, the afternoon was turning dark and the streetlights lit the street.

John casually reached down and scooped up a handful of snow, then made it into a snowball.

"Great snow," he told me, and I knew what he meant.

I grabbed some snow of my own and saw that he was right. You could tell just by the feel of the snow — wet and heavy — that it was perfect for making snowballs and snow forts. As I squeezed the snow into a ball, it made that squeaking sound, always a good sign for snowball-makers.

"See what I mean?" he asked. But before I could answer, he had lobbed his snowball at me, hitting me in the chest.

"Hey!" I yelled through my grin as he backpedaled away from me, scooping snow as he went.

He laughed and pointed at me just as I whipped my first snowball at him. With a nifty move, he sidestepped my snowball.

"Call that a throw?" he asked, firing a snowball my way.

I ducked and returned fire. The war was on!

And it continued as the afternoon turned dark, with us zigzagging in the driveway, across the lawn, down the street, laughing all the time.

"Truce," I finally called, as I caught my breath. "We probably should go in."

"Okay," John said, yanking his hat off his sweaty head.

As we walked up the street toward our driveway, he flung a fistful of snow over his shoulder at me, catching me in the face. Before I could say anything, he was dashing up the driveway. I wasn't going to let him get away with that.

In a flash, I made a snowball and fired it at him. At the last second he turned and noticed my incoming rocket. With a grin, he ducked, and the snowball sailed past him and, to my horror, headed toward the front of the house next door, where my Uncle Walter lived. It was one of those slow-motion moments, when events slow down but you are still powerless to change anything.

My snowball scored a direct hit, right in the center of the three plastic choir boys who were standing with O-shaped mouths in front of my uncle's house. With a crack, the chest of the boy in the middle opened up revealing a large white Christmas bulb, like a heart.

"Oh, no," I cried, checking to see if my uncle came to the door. "What should we do?"

Without hesitation, my brother answered, "Run!"

And we did. Up the hill, then we cut through the Ruffinos' yard and came out on Marlboro Road. Huffing and puffing, we walked slowly down the street.

"Holy mackerel," I said. "I can't believe it."

"Yeah," John said with a cackle, "nice shot."

"Do you think anybody saw us?"

He shrugged. "I guess we'll find out at the party."

I didn't know what to say as we hurried down the street, then cut through Hansens' yard into our own backyard.

"Just in time," my mother said. "Go get cleaned up. Company will be here any minute."

We returned to the living room in ten minutes, faces pink and clean, to see the room beginning to fill up with aunts and uncles and cousins. But what made me stop dead was my father talking to my Uncle Walter in the hall. As I walked by, I heard my uncle say, "I bet it was one of those high school hooligans that did it, threw that snowball right through my ornament."

"You're probably right," my father said as he looked at me, "but you never know."

Was my face on fire or did it just feel that way?

I hurried into the kitchen and told John what I had heard.

"Don't worry about it."

I told him about the look our father had given me.

"Don't worry about it," he said again, this time a bit less confidently.

No matter what my brother told me, I did worry about what I had done. Not enough to confess to my father or to my uncle. But I did the next best thing.

The following evening when my parents went grocery shopping, I emptied my ceramic cowboy bank of all the change it held. I didn't even count it. I slid it into a small white envelope that I took from my mother's desk. Then I sneaked over to my uncle's front door and laid the envelope on the front porch. I gave the white envelope a little pat, then hurried home.

CHAPTER FIFTEEN

Writing a Descriptive Essay

in 1969 as the brainchild
vanted to open a recordi
illage in upstate New Yo
Bob Dylan. The businessm
attract a lot of attention
metown. Although they h
s to risk money on t
vestors were interested
of this project that was
Music and Art F
Days of Peace a
t accommodate
end the fair, t
e was move
nsidered wh
passing any "m
lence" (American
peace singers like A
her acts were soon
rformers read like a
luding the Grateful D
arwater Revival, and
o took pains to plan f
cilities, and a medical st
t went into Woodstoc

Writing a descriptive essay gives you a great chance to watch. That may not seem very exciting, but it is the basis for writing a good descriptive essay. If you do not look carefully at your subject — be it a tree house, your grandfather's woodworking shop, or a ride at Disneyland — you are not going to be able to include vivid and accurate details in your essay. And no one wants to read an essay that is filled with vague phrases like "it's pretty big" or "the saw makes a funny sound." That's just not good writing.

There is a difference between writing a report about a place — for example, my sample report on Scotland on page 117 of this guide — and writing a descriptive essay about a place. The difference is in the purpose of the writing. In a report about a place, you are trying to convey facts that you gained through research, either in print or online or from interviews and videos. In a personal essay, on the other hand, you're writing to share your personal observations and your feelings about a place.

When you write about a place, you need to be ready to find details that appeal to the five senses: sight, sound, smell, taste, and touch. And, in addition to the senses, you also need to be aware of a feeling that you get from a place. You might, for example, feel safe and comfortable when you are in your grandfather's shop. You get that feeling because of the way the place affects your senses. Maybe it's the warmth of the heater and the smell of freshly sawed wood that does the trick. So, when you write about a place, pay attention to your senses and to the way the place makes you feel.

Getting ideas

When you're ready to observe, make sure you have a notebook and pencil by your side. You might start by making a list of possible subjects, perhaps places from memory or places that you can actually visit and take notes about. Spend a little time walking around your neighborhood noticing things. Do some observing at school or around your house or apartment. Look for places that mean something to you. Good writing is easier when you, the writer, are really interested in the subject.

If you take a look at the activities I suggested at the start of Chapter Fourteen (see pages 195 to 203), you will find that many of them can help you get some ideas for a descriptive essay. For example, you might write a personal essay about a place in your neighborhood where you and your friends hung out; your closet or the cellar of your house; the vet's office, where you frequently visited with your pet; a place that you associate with one of your grandparents; the place you go to when you want to be alone; or some place in the town where you used to live that you can't replace in your new town.

Don't forget that you are looking for a place that means a great deal to you, but it can be a place you don't enjoy visiting, like the orthodontist's office or assistant principal's office.

If you want to write about a place from your memory, you will need to make sure you can recall it in vivid detail. One way to help you recall places from your memory is to write "I REMEMBER" at the top of a page in your notebook and try to complete that thought. You may very well remember places. When you do, write them down, as well as whatever information your memory gives you. But you don't need to rely totally on your memory. If you are writing about last summer's vacation trip to Disneyland, for example, you might ask your family for some help remembering details about the theme park. In fact, your parents and siblings might enjoy reliving that vacation trip. When they are ready to share their recollections, make sure you are ready to take notes. You might also want to look at some vacation snapshots or a videotape of the trip. Looking at pictures will not only give you concrete images, but it may also trigger some of your own memories. Remember that you're looking for specific details that will allow you to share your personal impressions with your reader.

When you are looking for a subject for an essay about a place, remember two things: Think small and make it personal. In other words, don't try to write a short essay on Disneyland. There are whole books (and reports!) on the subject. Instead, focus on your impressions of the park. What was your favorite ride? Why? What do you remember about it? Was there a section of the park that you liked more than other parts? Why? Be ready to show someone what your topic means to you. If you are looking for ideas closer to home, don't write about your house. Write about your room. The writing model that I wrote for this chapter, for example, is about a tree house, not about the entire backyard.

Getting Organized

Since it's important to include details that appeal to the senses in a good descriptive essay, you might want to begin your brainstorming by listing details of your subject. But, more than that, you want to make sure that you also include details on how the place made you feel. To help me organize all these details for my writing model on a tree house, I used a sense chart and filled in these details in the appropriate places.

➡ SIGHT: triangular platform, each side about six feet long, wooden slats, railing, unpainted

➡ SOUND: yelling during our games, pulley and bucket, mosquitoes

➡ SMELL: cats in sand pile

➡ TASTE: (There are no taste details for this essay.)

➡ TOUCH: rough boards, swaying in wind

➡ FEELING: safe and comfortable with my friends

A chart like the one I used above helped me to get a clear image of the tree house, but I wanted my essay to do more than that. I needed to find the best way to include clear details that involve the senses while I tell the story of why the tree house meant so much to me.

A Word About Craft

Modifiers

A good way to vary your sentences is to begin some of them with phrases and clauses. However, you need to be careful about the modifiers you use at the beginning of a sentence. When you start a sentence with a phrase or a clause, the word or group of words that follows the comma should be related to that phrase or clause. Take a look at this sentence: "Exhausted by the long flight, a good night's sleep sounded good." What this sentence really says is that "a good night's sleep" was "exhausted by the long flight." But we know that's not what the sentence intended to say. So, we can rewrite that sentence this way: "Exhausted by the long flight, I looked forward to a good night's sleep." Here are two more examples:

1. "While driving through the park, my rear tire went flat."
   Revised: "My rear tire went flat while I was driving through the park."

2. "Thumbing through the book, the colorful diagrams were noticed."
   Revised: "Thumbing through the book, she noticed the colorful diagrams."

Writing the Draft

Before you begin writing your draft, you should have a pretty good idea about which details you're going to include in the body of your essay. However, don't forget to give some thought to the introduction and the conclusion of the essay. Your introduction should get the reader's attention and let her know what the topic of your essay is going to be. In my sample essay, I begin with a story about a going-away party that got me thinking about what I would miss if I had to leave my house. The introduction paragraph ends with this sentence: "The more I thought about it, the more I realized how much I would miss my tree house in the far corner of our backyard." This sentence clearly signals to the reader what she will be reading in my essay.

The conclusion of your descriptive essay should bring your piece of writing to a clear end. You don't want your reader to feel disappointed that you abruptly stopped writing. In the concluding paragraph to my sample essay I include a sentence that mentions the points that I included in the essay: " . . . it's a special place filled with many memories of good friends and good times." I hope that my conclusion will leave the reader satisfied with the end of the essay.

Your draft should be more than a cut-and-dry description. You can go beyond simple description in your essay by showing the heart of the place you're describing. How do you do that? In my writing model, I describe the basic structure of the tree house, but then I include a couple of paragraphs that describe some of the special features that made this tree house so neat. Then I spent a paragraph showing how I felt in the tree house, followed by a paragraph that describes some of the memories attached to it. It's these little "extras" that give a heart to the description.

As you write your draft, look at the sense details and try to find a way to go beyond them to show what your subject means to you. Yes, you want to include details, but you also want to make sure your reader can understand why the place you're writing about is so important to you.

Revision Checklist

→ Do you think your reader will get a feel for the place you're describing? Can you point to a few spots that convey that feeling? If not, look for a way to show what the place means to you.

→ Do you have details that appeal to the senses? Do you include details that make the place memorable?

→ Does your introduction grab the reader's attention?

→ Do you make sure your modifiers are placed near the words that they relate to?

The other day after school, there was a small party in a corner of the school cafeteria. Some other boys and I got together to say good-bye to a boy who had only been in our class since the beginning of the year. But because his father was in the military, he had to move again. He didn't seem very sad about moving. I guess he was used to it by now. But it got me thinking about how I would feel if I had to move. I know I would really hate moving for a lot of reasons, like leaving my friends, the ball field, and my house. The more I thought about it, the more I realized how much I would miss my tree house in the far corner of our backyard.

My father built it about six years ago, before I was ready for it, and it's not much to look at. It is a wooden triangular platform nailed to three trees. Each side of the triangle is about six feet long. A railing about chest-high runs around the platform. Wooden slats go from the railing to the floor of the tree house. The platform, railing, and slats are all rough wood, and none of the surfaces are painted. A ladder hangs on the tree at the corner of the tree house closest to our house.

Actually, Dad still hasn't gotten around to finishing the tree house. A side and a half of the railing still have no slats attached to them. But that's okay because that is where my friends and I added our special touches. From one open side we attached a slide from an old swing set, and from the other opening we hung a rope ladder.

The tree house has some other neat features that I have added over the years. I attached a small pulley and a rope to the railing, which I can use to haul up a bucket that we often fill with camping gear or snacks. I also strung a rope to a tree about three feet from one corner of the tree house. I hang wet clothes or signal flags on the line. Underneath the tree house is a pile of sand from an old sandbox. My friends and I used to have fun playing in that sandpile until Beezer, the neighbor's cat, and some of his friends started using it as a litter box!

Because Dad didn't want the tree house too high, it is only about six feet off the ground. Still, it's easy to get the feeling that you are much higher up in the trees. The trees that the platform is attached to are large elms. This means that whenever the wind is blowing hard, the tree house will move just enough to give you the feeling that you're on a raft riding the ocean swells.

Even though my tree house might not be much to look at, it is the memories of playing in it with my friends that make the place special. At one time or another, the tree house was a jungle outpost and we were brave explorers. The mosquitoes added a nice touch! So did our poodle, who became a raging tiger chasing us. When the wind was really blowing, we were pirates flying the Jolly Roger as we sailed the seven seas. There was no end to what our imaginations could help us become whenever we were in that tree house.

I don't play in the tree house too much since I started middle school. Still, it is a good place to go when I want to be by myself. But more than that, it's a special place filled with many memories of good friends and good times. Every time I look out my bedroom window and see the tree house, I am reminded of how lucky I am.

CONCLUSION
Writing in Your Life

Students frequently ask me, "Why do you write?" That's a good question because we need to ask ourselves why we do what we do, especially if we spend a lot of time doing it. I usually tell students, "I write because I like it." That may seem like a lame answer, but it's true. There is so much I like about putting words on paper, whether I'm writing a poem or a chapter for a book like this one. Oh, it's hard work sometimes, I can't deny that. But most of the time I forget about the hard work when I write something that satisfies me.

Another thing I like about writing is learning as I write. Sometimes I learn when I do research, as I did when I wrote the reports in this guide. (I love going to the library, any library.) But, beyond that, I learned more about writing by writing this guide. So, as I wrote and revised (and revised again!), I learned more about how to write better.

Writing is a skill, like playing third base. You don't get to be a better third baseman by having nice hair. You get to be a better third baseman by practicing taking ground balls and throwing to first. Don't forget to practice your writing.

Being a good writer will help you in school, of course, when you have writing assignments, like writing an essay for a standardized test. But writing can also help you be a more careful thinker throughout your life. I see the truth in what William Faulkner, one of the great American novelists said, "I never know what I think about something until I read what I've written."

I hope that some of the things that I included in this guide help you to be a better writer. I think you'll find that writing well is fun, even though it is hard work at times. If you ask me, writing's a great deal. It's a rush knowing that what you write on a page can touch other people. It can make them laugh or cry. It can persuade them. It can let them remember. It can inform them. That's the power of your words. Maybe that's another reason why I write — to feel the power of my words. I hope this guide helps you to feel your own power.